O R D I N A R Y
T I M E

ORDINARY TIME

Stories of the
Days between
Ascensiontide
and Advent

Phyllis A. Tickle

THE UPPER ROOM
Nashville, Tennessee

Ordinary Time

No part of this book may be used or reproduced in any manner whatsoever without written permission of the publisher except in brief quotations embodied in critical articles or reviews. For information address The Upper Room, 1908 Grand Avenue, P.O. Box 189, Nashville, TN 37202.

"Of Bulls and Angels" first appeared in HOMEWORDS: A BOOK OF TENNESSEE WRITERS (Knoxville: The University of Tennessee Press, 1986) and is used with permission of the publisher.
"Haying" first appeared, in slightly different form, in THE CITY ESSAYS (Memphis: The Dixie Flyer Press, 1982) and is used here with permission of the publisher, as is "To My Pear Trees."

First Printing: February 1988 (5)
Library of Congress Catalog Card Number: 87-051427
ISBN: 0-8358-0575-1

Printed in the United States of America

CONTENTS

ORDINARY
TIME

PROLOGUE

HOLY SEASONS, LIKE HOLY DAYS, WERE NOT SO
much invented by the church as they were invented
by life itself, I think. By common consent we hold to
and preserve that which living has shown us contains
the truths of both humankind and God.

I am not a cleric. I have never wanted to study in a
seminary or even to have access to one. I am instead
a layperson, a writer and editor by trade, a woman.
Over my fifty-odd years of living in cities and vil-
lages, mill towns and on farms, I have come increasingly to think that every believer must be a kind of
psalmist, either literally or privately. That living itself
has been given, at least in part, as a way of knowing
God intimately. Every event takes on significance in
that context, for there is no waste in experience.
Every man and woman we meet becomes a metaphor of ourselves; every event, a simile; every thing,
a symbol.

As Christians we are taught that our collective
understanding and knowledge over the centuries since
the coming of God have become, and are contained
in, the liturgy and ritual of the church herself, the
body of Christ passing itself on to each new member—
part in the spiritual codes of symbol and sacrament,
ritual and saint. Increasingly I find hope of the
shared symbol's becoming once more the common
language by which we rear our young, and the

mother tongue by which we all will someday cut the lines that separate us from one another.

The essays which follow are true in that they factually report what has happened to me and my family during the days of many holy seasons past. I hope they are true to the mark also in that, in retelling one family's progress toward liturgical truth, they will represent the progress of many, many families toward that same understanding.

We live in a culture still too new to yet have defined itself and under a government so young that my own lifetime has spanned a quarter of its history. In such times and circumstances I have found, in the heritage of the church, a transcendent purpose and connectedness for my own part of creation. For that I have always been grateful. This book is dedicated to the hope that it may be so also for my own children and for those fellow Christians for whom Christianity is both our past and our future.

—From the Prologue to
What the Heart Already Knows

INTRODUCTION

*An Introduction to the Days between
Ascensiontide and Advent*

No SEASON OF THE CHURCH'S CALENDAR AND no portion of its liturgy begin with more confusion than does the seventh and last part of the sacred year, those final twenty-five, –six or –seven weeks that stretch from Ascensiontide through to Advent.

Suffice it to say that all Christians seem to agree that the Ascension of Our Lord took place forty days after His Resurrection. We all also seem to hold in common agreement the celebration of Pentecost. Pentecost—no more than a Greek word lifted directly into our language and meaning "fifty"—comes ten days after Ascension. Simple so far.

If one thinks about it arithmetically, one realizes without even looking at a lectionary or a service book that Ascension must always come on Thursday, since Easter always comes on Sunday. One also calculates very readily the fact that the Sunday after Ascension is still part of the Great Fifty Days of Easter. The following Sunday, however, is the tricky one.

The Sunday after the Sunday after the Ascension is Pentecost. It plainly and clearly falls fifty days after Easter and fulfills its semantic obligation to be fifty. It is also the day on which the tongues of flame descended on the assembled Apostles; the day when Holy Ghost dramatically entered the church's history

11

by occupying the bodies of the believers; the day when those around the assembled were convicted and converted by what they saw with their eyes and heard with their ears.

In its own way, Pentecost's story is the most compelling one in our faith. Christ is gone, removed, triumphantly absent. Now life—human, humdrum, secular life—must end its mourning, hang up its miracles, question its memories. And History would have done all those things . . . would have helped life to erode its one truth . . . except for Pentecost. On that day in one singular event the nature of humanity, or of some among humanity, is publicly reconstituted so as to house the nature of God . . . and History is relegated to being a tool instead of a cause. Strong stuff in anybody's book, and one cannot really blame the church for having treated the results a bit gingerly, to say the least.

Without incarnate God and resurrected Lord, certainly, Pentecost would not have happened. But it is a prudent believer who always knows, twenty-four hours a spiritual day, that were it not for Pentecost, both the Incarnation and the Resurrection would have been unreceivable, would have been remembered longings, as poignant and useless as our memories of flying during the naps and dreams of infancy.

Pentecost hooked us up to the myth. It put the myth inside and made it fact for the soul. It became, thereby, the Great Miracle; it became also everyone's miracle, the possession of each believer and the most intimate chamber of mystery.

And because we fear it, or so I have always thought, we have always fought it. We have fought it and wrestled with it in myriad ways that must surely have amused our nonbelieving friends over the centuries and furnished them with yet more reasons to question our claim to be the people of God.

We have, for instance, tried varying its name, but each time the new name has turned on us to speak of even starker truths. Centuries ago, for instance, in England, the day itself was often called "Whitsunday" from the Old English word for "white." *The White Sunday* . . . how startlingly accurate is the terror of that name! Out of it grew Whitsuntide, the now-almost-lost liturgical season of Anglicanism that lasted only for a calendar week from White Sunday until the following Sunday, called always "Trinity Sunday."

And Trinity Sunday became a whole new way for our religious forebears to fight with the mysteries they feared. They came to call the weeks after Trinity Sunday . . . or after Whitsunday . . . or after Whitsuntide . . . or after Pentecost (it's your personal choice here) . . . they came to call those twenty-five-odd weeks the "season of Trinity." The irony was, of course, that the concept of monotheistic Trinity is one of the most difficult of the mysteries celebrated in the season, and once again humanity's desire to divert was thwarted by God's intention to be heard.

As a result, the church in its various denominational parts has developed various denominational ways to label and/or calculate the days that stretch from Ascensiontide to Advent. The Episcopalian tradition out of which I come, for instance, has recently resumed its former ways of numbering. Now, the weeks of what I have always called "Trinity" (the season, that is) are named by how far they are from

Pentecost. Thus, Whitsunday is rarely mentioned at all anymore, but Pentecost is; and thus the first Sunday after Pentecost is Trinity, but the second Sunday of old Trinity is now more usually called the "Third Week after Pentecost."

If all of this is not wonderfully instructive or even very important, in and of itself, I contend that the confusion it evidences and the strong resistance it bespeaks are significant. Anytime any process becomes this cluttered and belabored, one can bet that there is a reason. But why does naming or even calculating a sacred season matter at all?

It matters because every religion must have its canon of mysteries. All of ours, save Incarnation and Resurrection, are tucked into those twenty-five-odd weeks, and it makes us quite nervous that it should be so.

Religion's mysteries, in order to be effective, must deal very specifically with reality and variant reality; that is the function of mysteries. Christianity's needs in that regard are the same as those of any other religion from the most primitive animism to the most sophisticated Buddhism.

Many a man or woman would also like to say that because human nature is human nature, the variants of reality that a religion must address will be the same from the most primitive animism to the most sophisticated Buddhism. If it were not for Pentecost, the Christian could agree. Unfortunately, however— at least from the secularist's point of view—the Christian cannot say that, because it is known by that Christian, by the church, and by every other Christian that Christian human nature was changed at Pentecost.

The penultimate result of Pentecost is that now the God in us is God looking at God—an exercise, at least for those who have passed through their own Pentecost, a little like trying to see into one's own eyes or bite one's own teeth, to use Alan Watts's analogy. And that's a hard bill of goods to sell, much less explain.

And finally, the most current result of all this confusion and this history of wrestling with paradox to extract its truth lies in a fairly recent decision by the Roman church and some Protestant churches. Very few things have helped all of us more than that decision to call the time from Pentecost to Advent by a new name . . . to call it "Ordinary Time."

As a name for a liturgical season—for half the calendar year, in fact—Ordinary Time, too, is stark in its simplicity, for, as we all know, there is no such thing.

ST. BARNABAS

ST. BARNABAS WAS THE MOST HUMBLE AND THE most unself-acclaimed of the major saints. As a result, he is also the most obscure, known more for the results of his life than for himself. It is gloriously appropriate, consequently, that he should be the saint whose feast day is always the first to be celebrated in Trinity.

There is no idea more characteristic of Trinity than the idea of paradox, and few ideas are more paradoxical than the notions of losing one's life in order to find it; of selling all that one has in order to be wealthy; of making oneself invisible in order to be potent in one's presence. And Barnabas, of all the original Christian community, was the one who lived out all three contradictions—lived them to the hilt, as my children say.

Originally Barnabas was probably the wealthiest of the fellowship. Certainly we know that he was the handsomest. We also know that his name was really Joseph and that he was a Levite, a native of Cyprus. His sister was supposedly one of the inner circle of women who surrounded Jesus during His lifetime. We also know that her son (and, thereby, Joseph's nephew) was John Mark, the gospeler and the sometimes companion of St. Paul on his missionary journeys. In fact, it was over Mark that Joseph and Paul were eventually to differ and separate (thus spreading the faith in two directions instead of in one, I

might add; the kind of result that's typical of everything our saint did or tried to do).

We first meet him, not during Jesus' lifetime, but
after Pentecost when, with the others, he lingers in
Jerusalem waiting for some plan or direction. In
those first untroubled weeks of unanimity and ecsta-
sy, the Apostles and believers enjoyed the kind of
total harmony that would never come again to the
church on earth and that was destined to be fleeting
even while they had it.

The custom during this brief respite from reality
was for the early converts to sell all that they owned,
convert it to cash, and give the money to the Apostles for use among the poor. Of those who gave their
goods in this way, we know the names of only three:
Joseph, the Cypriot Levite, whose gift was effective;
and Ananias and his wife, Sapphira, whose gift, cursed
by their greed, brought them instantaneous death at
Peter's feet. In that dramatic little piece of business,
the church had its first apostasy and its first crisis.

It is entirely typical of the Cypriot that his genuine
self-effacement should end up for all time in such
sharp and devastating juxtaposition to the self-serving
ways of the doomed Ananias and Sapphira. His whole
life, in fact, is the story of a man trying to throw
himself away for his Lord and always getting back
more than he had thrown. No wonder then that the
Apostles came in time to surname him Barnabas, a
name that stuck to him and that means both "the son
of exhortation" and "the son of consolation." And no
wonder either that he should, in spite of his best
efforts toward invisibility, still be the saint who most
frequently opens the door to Trinity for us.

1.

ABOUT GARBAGE AND REDEMPTION

You HAVE TO UNDERSTAND ABOUT COUNtry garbage to understand about last St. Barnabas Day.

It was one of those clear, light, almost-not-there days when everything is easy because there are no boundaries, no divisions in the world. The inside was as cool and as warm as the outside. All the doors were open and all the windows raised, but it wouldn't have mattered if they hadn't been. The freshness would have found us anyway, traveling as it was on slides of sunlight through everything. School was out, and there were no schedules to keep. The children's freedom was still recent enough so that it was not yet a burden to them or to me. A golden day set in the middle of a golden week.

Holy days, when they fall during the week, are usually observed at midmorning and at eventide in the country, so ten o'clock and St. Barnabas was our first and only obligation beyond enjoyment this day, except for taking the garbage to the dump; and that, too, is a kind of enjoyment for me, an adventure.

John had loaded the barrels into the truck the night before and put the tarp over them, lashing the whole with his own, very solid brand of roping so that the tarp wouldn't flap and tear. We were definitely a truckload of country garbage on its way to the dump, but we were going to be a neat load of country garbage, nonetheless.

When we first came to the farm to live, we used a dump that was no more than a quarter of a mile down the highway from our church. So long as that dump was active, it was a common sight on non-Sunday holy days to see several pickup trucks loaded with garbage barrels in the church parking lot during midmorning services. Much to our private regret, however, the landfill filled up about four years ago, and we are now forced to go five miles farther north past the church to a new county dump. It's every bit as interesting as the old one, of course; just farther away for us and nearer for most of our fellow parishioners. The most obvious result of this shift in the scheme of things is that now our fellow worshipers don't bring their garbage to church; we still do.

Now if there's anything in the world that upsets a fifteen-year-old, it's being different. And being different, like everything else, has its gradations, the agony of each adolescent being in direct proportion to the remarkable degree of his differentness. Thus, since we were the only communicants routinely hauling our truckload of refuse to holy days, John had developed a genuine reluctance toward both religion and trash. Because I strongly believe that adolescent boys are better haulers and toters of fifty-gallon drums than are their mothers, he and I were not infrequently at loggerheads about why we were taking the garbage yet again and about why he was going with me when we did it. His strong protests that I used to do it alone when he was little and that I would have to do it again as soon as he and Sam, Jr., were grown were entirely irrelevant to the parent in charge, namely, me.

So grumbling and honestly compromised (I was not totally insensitive to his position), he, Becca, and Sam, Jr., trooped out to the truck. Trying to wedge myself into the cab with them, I realized that our days of disposing of garbage this way were being numbered by their growing bulk, but I was not about to say so, much less give John the satisfaction of any hope just yet. So, grateful to the core that it was an easy day, I cranked us up and away we went to St. Barnabas.

The service that morning was remarkably unre-markable. Barnabas has been a favorite of mine ever since someone told me, years ago when I was a child, the story of his missionary trip to Antioch. The Antiochians were so taken with his good looks and handsome physique that they thought he was Jupiter, king of the gods. In fact, so the story goes, they almost sacrificed a cow and some incense to him before he managed to stop them. That image, that palpable sensation of being even briefly seen as godlike and worthy of sacrificial homage, so moved my childish ego that I have loved old Barnabas ever since. As an adult I have certainly been curious about what kind of grace makes a Barnabas tick.

Anyway, the homily that morning, just as on every other St. Barnabas Day of my life, had been full of religion and none of the poetry of having a face and a body that look like they belong to the king of the gods. *It was an awful shame*, I thought, and the observances had been, as a result, also an awful shame.

When we came out of church forty-five minutes

later, the world had warmed up a bit. In fact it was hot, and the cab downright overheated under the midmorning sun. We climbed into our forced intimacy, and windows all rolled down, wind blowing and tarp holding, we hit the highway and the fifty-five-mile-an-hour ride to the dump. Much as I love air-conditioned cars, the joy of near racing just doesn't happen without that extra stimulus of wind and grit in my face. The needle went to sixty and was approaching sixty-five when Rebecca said, "Mama!" Sometimes I think that she's the oldest and staidest child in the world. No romance of the open road and all of that in the child at all. But I did slow us back down. The barrels and Becca sighed with relief, and the boys grinned. They at least can always be counted on to like the race to the dump . . . once we have cleared the church parking lot.

The man who runs the new dump is a dour sort of fellow. One has to have a rather particular kind of world view to run a dump, I imagine, and I enjoy eliciting his from time to time. You do not have conversations with this man, of course. He doesn't have that many words per customer in his daily allotment, but he is always good for a brief—one or two sentences maximum—assessment of you or your garbage and/or that of the driver and truck that just left.

Of all the semiconversations we have had in our three years of speaking to each other, and of all the situations I have seen him rise to, two—both dramatic, to say the least—stick in my mind as indicative of the man. The first is the time I saw him unexpectedly draw a pistol out of his shirt and take the head off a rat twenty yards away. "Ain't been no rats in this dump so far and ain't ever going to be" was his one-sentence summation of that event. Sure enough, I've not seen another rat since then, although I still think a pistol a rather extreme, if not expensive, solution to the problem; but a man who takes pride in his work is entitled, I suppose, to his own choice of methods.

My second commanding memory is of the day some poor soul backed too near to the edge of the dump shelf and slid right in—truck, barrels, and all. It took the bulldozer and a dozen of us onlookers to pull the fellow out. "Shoulda left the durned fool down there if he's that blind" was the summation on that one. "Downright dangerous to have folks like that on the roads these days ... 'sides he smells to holy heaven now." And leaving the bulldozer's huge motor idling, he was gone to direct another pickup into place on the shelf.

So it was not unusual on a warm and slow day for him to come and greet us, which he did that morning. He then usually stood and watched wordlessly while the boys dumped the barrels, which he also was doing that morning. One barrel dumped. Sam moved the second forward, and John tilted it over. The third moved to the tailgate, and John bent to tilt it.

"'Scuse me, Lady, but I think you've throwed away your cat."

It was so laconic, so matter-of-factly factual, that neither the boys nor I reacted at first. John tipped the third barrel as if nothing had been said, and then just as he tilted the load beyond recall, we all three registered what we had just been told. And there, beneath John's cascade of falling garbage, was Alouette, scrambling up through rotten peels, soggy rags, and old cans, one kitten still dangling drunkenly from her mouth.

I hollered. John hollered. Sam, Jr., hollered. John jumped off the tail, Sam vaulted over the side, and I took off running. She made it halfway down the shelf before we caught her. The kitten, not more than twelve hours old, was frantic by the time John got it separated from Alouette's jaws and began to cuddle it. Alouette, for her part, fought me every step of the way back up to the truck, turning and slapping at me as we climbed. I held her at arm's length and hollered at Becca to close the cab windows and get ready to receive one mad cat. John put the kitten on the floor at Becca's feet, and I set Alouette on top of it, slamming the door as fast as I could behind her.

Then we started the sorting of the piles we had just made, following the mewing as it led us to kitten after kitten. Each time we unburied one, we beat on the cab for Becca to crack a window enough for us to hand in another kitten. It was not until we had found and reclaimed all six of them that Alouette was content to stay unrestrained in the cab with Becca. By that time all four of us were dripping with sweat and dust, the boys and me from clambering through garbage and exertion, and Rebecca from being shut up in the steaming cab with the cat family.

The boys made fast work of the remaining barrels, except one we left half full so that Alouette and her family could be reinstalled as soon as we could get back home with them and their nursery of choice. We rolled up the tarp and lashed the empty barrels in. Becca held Alouette's nape while the boys and I crawled back into the cab. Through the closed window, I waved our thanks to the overseer still standing there propped against his dozer. He raised his hand, and through the glass, I heard him say, "Bye, Lady. See you next time." Then, "Better make them boys take a bath, though. They smell to holy heaven." Beside me John died yet another adolescent death, and wise old Rebecca said, "It may stink in here, but at least you won't go so fast with the windows up."

Suddenly I started laughing. In less than one hour's time we had gone from mass to this, and the contrast was just too much for me. I had an image of Barnabas with his body like the king of the gods looking down at us so newly and so odorously come from his commemorative day. What a chuckle he must be getting out of this holy day...and what a chuckle he must have gotten out of his own first "holy" day! To have some benighted soul come up and try to lay a heifer open, guts and all, at your feet must, like sorting garbage to retrieve kittens, tend to put lots of things in perspective for one, and rather quickly, too. It certainly would give one a sense of humor about the human condition. And that was what the sermons had never said in all those years. Barnabas had had a sense of humor. He must have. It was the only thing that made any sense. I sobered.

"Hey, kids, would you mind if I named one of the kittens Barnabas?"

They didn't. Of course they didn't know why either, but they let me do it anyway. He's sitting out there now on the patio, watching me; grooming his thick fur; holding court for me through the window; reminding me that sometimes, as a special grace, we still can find a part of our soul's salvation wrapped in the gift of laughter.

ST. PETER AND
ST. PAUL

ALTHOUGH NO ONE WISHES TO DENY EACH of the early Apostles and believers his or her just due, few historians would quarrel with the notion that Christianity was spread beyond the city limits of Jerusalem primarily through the zeal of three men: Paul, Barnabas, and Peter. The church's recognition of that partnership is demonstrated in its placing their feast days near each other in the liturgical calendar. And the church's recognition of the transfer of the kingdom to human hands after Pentecost is demonstrated by its opening Trinity with the feasts of the three most effective missionaries.

2.

PETER, PAUL, AND GRANNY

THE REAL REASON WE LIVE IN THE COUNTRY is that there is no longer a city anywhere that would ever let us store and house all the material goods Sam requires in order to feel secure and complete in this life. Not only is the man a keeper and saver, he is also a worrier. He is the kind who is absolutely sure that someday the cataclysm will come and we will be caught without everything that, had we been morally responsible, we would have stockpiled in order to survive it.

During the Cuban Missile Crisis I had the only cellar in the state of South Carolina that could have sustained life for a full year for a family of five, including the requisite supply of bottled water... and also the string, pins, needles, waste disposal sacks, razor blades, pencils and so on that such a year would require. We could have lived more comfortably in the cellar that year than we did upstairs like normal people, as a matter of fact.

But that is going on thirty years ago now, and all that the intervening years have done is increase the clutter and hone Sam's habits to a pitch of consummate perfection. We now have everything and can face any eventuality—except that of running out of space to store it all.

When we came here to the farm ten years ago,

there were only a barn and one outbuilding for storage. The barn looked immense to me, and I sighed a sigh of release from both anxiety and embarrassment; we would never fill it up (want to bet?) and no one could see us (much less watch us) while we tried.

In all honesty I have to admit that the barn was vacant when we moved. Six weeks later, however, with a full herd and their supplies installed, the barn was considerably less impressive. Nonetheless, since we were coming from a normal city house on a normal city lot (one that we had stretched to its fullest potential), the barn effectively absorbed all those things that had so compromised me in the city.

You see, what Sam, Sr., acquires and/or saves really is necessary rather than elegant. Years ago, for instance, he had torn down a back wall on our lot in the city; had carefully cleaned each of the bricks as he tore the thing down; and had carefully hauled each of those same bricks to the country with us when we moved... "a man can't ever tell when he will need a good brick or two." Now there's nothing wrong with that position as such, and there's nothing wrong with having a brick pile handy behind the barn. There had been, and always will be, a great deal wrong with having a brick pile at any spot in a city yard.

The same may also be said for a collection of thirty-two, gallon mayonnaise jars (that's eight cartons of four jars each, by the way) that may indeed be a great help someday. I haven't the faintest idea for what, but for something no doubt, especially since the man who gave them to him was, I was told, married to a spendthrift who simply could not see their potential and was being quite unreasonable about their presence in her city garage. They went quite nicely into the back stall of the barn and, for all I know, still sit there now awaiting their day of purpose.

The string-to-rope collection of everything that could ever be used to secure anything filled up all the corridor wall in the new barn; but it looked so much better there than it had in our city bedroom, kitchen, laundryroom, and den that I was overjoyed to walk through a corridor of cinctures every time I visited the cows that first summer. Likewise with the lengths of pipe, all of varying diameters, which, laid flat across the rafters, now constitute the ceiling for two paddocks of the barn—a solution infinitely better than having them propped on end randomly around the backyard fence in town.

In fact, one of my most portentous memories is of driving with Sam, one afternoon before we moved, through heavy city traffic. He pulled into an intersection and stopped for the light. Then, with an "Oh, my goodness!" he opened his door, leaned out into the street, and struggled to retrieve what turned out to be a length of pipe about two-and-a-half feet long and a half-inch in diameter. He was jubilant as he landed it successfully into the backseat before the light changed. It was typical of our relationship that I hadn't even seen the thing and that he chatted happily all the way home about how good it was to have yet another length of scrap conduit around the place. It was shortly after that that I begin to actively campaign for a move to the country.

Now, nearly a decade later, the barn has suffered certain additions . . . about forty feet protruding from its former front and about another forty protruding from its former back. It's a little hard to distinguish exactly where the old barn was or is, as the case may be, and it's a much longer walk than formerly to get anything out of the string-to-rope collection.

There is also a rather ungainly wooden thing near the barn. It's a bit too large to be a shed and a bit too awful to be a house, but it's full to its roofline with good stuff, all of it very good, in fact. We compromised our aesthetic differences, he and I, by painting the whole thing a flat, dull green that rather fades into the landscape for at least eight or nine months of the year.

The hen house, always an active place, has also been reengineered to allow for considerable storage. The hens originally seemed to share something of my point of view about any changes in their environment, but they proved to be equally ineffectual in getting things their way. So now they just live on resignedly with the gallon cans (uncounted) and the scraps of sheet metal as well as the chipped pottery that may someday be needed to start seedlings in.

The newest old structure is a compost house, or at least that's what it was when we came here. It has now been sealed up and roofed to become a weather-tight storage area for the lawn tractor, the bicycles, the hand mower, the hand tools, and the twenty-two shelves that came out of the old village store and will someday prove invaluable. The windows out of the store would not, however... I regret to say it... fit in the revamped compost house so they are propped outside against the back wall until we can figure where to build some structure or other in which they will once more be functional.

Now all of this I can tolerate in my husband because, first, there is some truth in the assertion that country living, unlike city living, really does require a considerable supply of ready-to-hand debris with which to patch and fix. We're too far out to get service reps to fix, either reasonably or quickly, most of what goes wrong; and we're much too far out to drive in for materials every time Sam has to fix whatever it was that did go wrong.

In the second place, and equally true, I knew before I got him that he was this way. His first cousin, in fact, never married because, by his own admission, he never could find a woman who would let him keep his plow on the front porch. So it's not as if I can say that I didn't know going in to this arrangement that he was one of those in whose hands frugality becomes a vice. I did.

And third, I suppose I must admit to a certain weakening on my part. It is nice to be able to get two bricks every time I want to protect a plant or prop a flowerpot. It's junky, but it's handy, a compromise I never could have imagined in myself ten years ago. How I, with all my years of fretting and protesting, could now have a place above the freezer for storing all the tinfoil pie plates that come in from the store is beyond me. I find it downright alarming, moreover, that I have a sizable section of the shop dedicated to storing various boxes and shipping containers that, who knows, I may need any day now for mailing something somewhere or for packing away something or for loading something into the car or a million other such possibilities.

But even allowing for my softening as well as for my foreknowledge, the truth still is that our life

together as a household has been one long exercise
in what my mother, while she was still alive and
living with us, used to call robbing Peter to pay Paul.
What she meant by this favorite aphorism was always
a mystery to the children when she would mutter it
under her breath with a shake of her head or offer it
to me as a logical device for family discussion. And
they would ask repeatedly what Grandma had against
Peter and which Peter was she talking about anyhow?

Applied to our case, of course, she simply meant
that given Sam's compulsion for always being prepared, we have always had to have increasing space
in which to store the essentials. The list of essentials
has always increased, of course, in direct proportion
to the expanding facilities and space which had to be
maintained so that they might store the required
essentials with which to maintain the expanding space,
et cetera, et cetera. It is a pattern that, as each child
has matured, he or she has come to recognize more
clearly in us and accept more charitably. Each has
also come to appreciate more completely the utility
of Granny's pet aphorism, so that now even twelve-
year-old Rebecca can apply it quite accurately to the
appropriate situations.

For instance, she came in yesterday afternoon
from her chores and asked me what happened when
Peter was robbed dry and Paul was too full to take on
more. Since I was in the middle of a serious casserole
and my mind was on ovens rather than philosophy, I
did a double take. What in the world was she talking
about?

"Well," she said, "since the barn goes all the way
to the edge of the pasture hillock in back now and all
the way to the garden gate in front and since we've

run out of sheds and the compost house is full, I just wonder what Daddy was going to do about Peter and Paul."

Before I could even think my way into the intricacies of her metaphor, I heard John behind me say, "Same as God did with the originals...pass it all on to us." He was propped against the hall door, just as he is at the same time every night, waiting for his dinner and indifferent to every concern except food.

"Yeah," said Becca as she set the fresh eggs into the sink and began to wash them, "then you better be sure you're as good a man as the originals."

For my part I was glad to be occupied with the casserole, strongly suspecting as I re-covered it that there was little that I or anyone else should add to the conversation.

JULY 4
INDEPENDENCE DAY

In its list of major feasts and services, the Episcopal Church in America has bowed only twice to secular holidays. One is Thanksgiving, and the other is Independence Day. Unlike any other parts of the secular calendar, both are by their very nature religious, if not specifically Christian. The giving of thanks becomes all men and enriches every experience. It is indeed good that we should give thanks unto the Lord, by whatever name we individually may call Him.

Likewise, freedom enriches us. Although it may not be used by all of us to practice the Christian faith, it does create full play for the checks and balances of human variety, for the oppositions and inconsistencies that make our society. It takes most of us no more than a week or certainly a fortnight outside our own borders to discover just how central the free play of human values is to our individual, as well as our civil, well-being.

But freedom has never been defined satisfactorily; and it is the constant honing of its definition, the shifting of the biases of its definers, the interchanges of tension between custom and progress, that make July 4 religious. No one can define freedom for oneself until one has defined one's god(s), one's own purposes, and the compromises one is willing to make to serve them both.

3.

TO MY PEAR TREES

After my bath I stay long in the tub, listening to the soft, cotton suck of the water as it circles the drain. I lie through that instant of near bursting when my bones take up the weight of my flesh again from the retreating water. I feel the vacuum as it pulls my back hard against the porcelain bottom, and as flat as if I were young again. My skin and hair release the water, droplet by droplet, to the gravity of air and drain, and I live briefly in the slow effervescence of their drying.

Even when it's finally gone, this will still be my water. It will come back again to me, to my body, to our house. It leaves now in copper pipes that run off into cool clay ones that in turn drain, just beyond the orchard fence, into the gravel overrun where, purified, it sinks slowly under the roots of grass, trees, and vines.

Some spring soon it will flower or make milk for a new calf; some fall soon it will drip from the juice of our pears or fatten a steer for market. This is water that leaves us only for a few seasons.

In its origin it is not our water, of course. City water was brought into this part of the country almost ten years ago, brought without the consent of those who farm here, brought in the name of the public good, and paid for by assessment of the unwilling. Our house, like the others in the community, had always been plumbed into its own well. When the water came, each one, ours included, had to be disconnected—severed from itself and reconnected to pipes whose names no one knew. In our homes water had become a manufactured necessity, a commodity to be produced elsewhere and transported at great expense to a dependent market.

The outside water is different. The water in the barn, the water in the hen house, the water in the hose pipes... that's our water... ours from our well and brought up by our pump. The houses may have had to be connected to utility pipes, but not the farms themselves. On the days when the utility company has the water shut off to repair the lines or even on the days when the pressure in the inside faucets is low, we can still trip the pump switch and draw up what is ours, what is not another's to shut off or treat or pollute. It is an independence that even the younger children, despite their hatred of summer watering chores, fiercely value.

Like me, they remember the hot days of two summers ago when the well went out; when we watched anxiously as their father climbed up and down, up and down, from the ground to the well-house roof, rigging a homemade derrick; when in that devastating heat of 105 degrees, he pulled the well-shaft by hand, inch after inch, until it stood a hundred feet above us like a prayer tower into the belly of heaven. They remember, too, the afternoon of the fourth day when, a new valve in place, he sank the shaft back into the water table; how we all stood waiting in the heat while he primed and primed and the water came racing out to the frantic fields and thirsty garden; how I cried when we saw it come; how he slapped them on the backs; how we had an early supper and an early bedtime; and how the water sang all night that night in the hose pipes.

It was not quite two months after that time of restoring that the machines came. They were a mile or so away from us, near the village; parked for a day or two, growing in number until there were seven of them—backhoes and Cats and two flatbeds of concrete pipe. On Thursday of the last week of September the stacks of ten-inch pipe were dropped, a dozen pipes per strapped bundle set out every thirty or forty feet along the roadside. On Saturday—on the day that should have been a free day—the crews came and began the digging. Backhoes along the edges of the road, backhoes into yards, backhoes crisscrossing the roadbed. It was suddenly two miles to get around them, two extra miles around the crisscrossing to the school and community center, two extra miles to the market where we sell our eggs. Sewers were coming! Once more, without having been asked or even told, we stood helplessly as the heavy equipment lumbered across us. The water we now had to pay to have hauled in was about to be wasted, hauled away, and we would have to pay for that, too. Our water was soon to pass totally through and beneath us in a sealed system of delivery as if it were a product and not a given.

The rains of October came, and the machines bogged down in the mud. We rejoiced when the great crustaceans were hauled away. All winter we hoped they would not come back to work the ditches. Of course they did, but times were hard, and there were fewer men, fewer machines, last summer. Only a dozen houses or so lost their last hold on the cycle of nature that had, since the beginning, nurtured them. As the fall ended and the winter began to move in, the machines were taken early to storage. They will come again next month or the one after that; eventually they will get us like they have gotten everyone else. So I lie long in this tub, feeling the water leave and sending it with love to my pear trees. How else, in what other way, can one mourn for the death of water, if indeed it is the water that is dying?

ST. MARY MAGDALENE

OF ALL THE WOMEN IN HOLY WRIT, MARY Magdalene is the most difficult to correctly assess and, therefore, to accurately honor. She is hardly the only prostitute in Scripture, if indeed she were one at all. Besides, even if we accept that job description for her, clearly Rahab the Harlot outdoes her for prominence and even for direct contribution to the historic events of the faith.

Mary is also scarcely traceable, for we know nothing of her lineage and almost nothing of her ending. But during the time of Christ's adult life, she was ubiquitous. From His earliest friendships to His resurrection scenes, there is Mary Magdalene. And that leads us to the question of *why*.

Why has been answered in at least two dozen different ways by literally hundreds of scholars and teachers over the centuries of talking about the Magdalene. Some of those answers are so sloppy and romantic as to be offensive as well as unworthy of the issue. Some of them are so shot through with theological burdens as to be intellectually effete as well as untenable. Basically, I think we do better by the Magdalene and her Lord if we take His word for it that only the sick have need of a doctor. That is, I think they were probably just friends, friends both because she was a sinner and because He was God.

Almost without fail, the company of people like the Magdalene is restorative and healing. Because they don't apply the rules to themselves, they have a wonderful tendency not to apply them to others. The resulting generosity of their viewpoint and of their conduct can refresh more deeply than any medicine I have ever taken.

It was to Mary, the all-accepting and the all-giving, then, that I think Christ must have turned frequently for human reinforcement. Hers was the kind of grace and openness of life that I will never have and that I can truly envy her; hers, a capacity for contact and nurture that we all would do well to consider if we, too, would keep company with her Christ. I came to this conclusion, by the way, not from any Bible study, but from experience.

4.

A PROMISE KEPT

I HAVE KNOWN TWO OF THEM IN MY LIFE-time—known them well and openly, that is. Probably even loved one of them, to the extent that our diverse schedules could grant any real existence to our affection. Any knowing at all is a bit of a fluke, I suspect, for a middle-class woman like me with a houseful of children and acceptable obligations. But apparently it was the writer side of me, and not the middle-class part, that each of them let in; the never-quite-fits-its-context side that each found paradoxical enough to accept.

Briefly, one of them—Vanna—even accepted me enough to participate, albeit distantly, in my family...at least to acknowledge that I had one...and to come once or twice to supper or a birthday party. But that was hard for her. Awkward. The kind of awkward that finally becomes indomitable, and we slipped back into the easier business of being together, just the two of us, in the daylight hours of our lives. We had met originally at a writers' conference, for she some-times still tried to support herself with free-lance reporting. But eventually, because there was no real reason for us to see each other routinely, the differ-ences in our lives began to erode our conversations and, in the end, our friendship.

But it was not like that with Bonnie. I can't even

remember now exactly how it was with Bonnie, but I can remember how it started...and how it ended. It was years ago. We were still living in the city, still struggling to build careers as well as children, and Grandma had just come to live with us that spring.

Bonnie was a beautician in some little hole-in-the-wall salon that had just opened and that I wandered into one day because it was there and I was tired. My hair is irascible in heat. (Since the rest of me is, too, I don't know why my hair shouldn't follow suit.) It kinks up, knots, flies, refuses to style, and generally burdens me with an awareness that it is there. Because it's that kind of hair, however, and nothing is going to make it look unobtrusive anyway, I can enjoy the luxury of a walk-in shampoo anytime I'm feeling the need for self-indulgence, and I was feeling it a lot that summer.

Walk in and walk out. The original drip-dry she called it that hot summer afternoon. That may have been what started it, what caught my attention. She certainly wasn't slick or posh or even ambitious as a beautician. That was probably what I understood first. She may have been the new owner of a small salon, but this wasn't her career, not really. I could sense it in everything about her. But the minute she touched my head, the minute those fingers began to move through my hair, I knew that whatever she really did or really was, she liked giving pleasure. She had that rare gift of knowing enough about her own body to understand someone else's...and the rare generosity that allowed her to give away her sensuality just as casually as she had received it.

I went back after that, time and again, even when it meant driving a city mile or two out of my way. I went for the joy of the shampoo certainly, and because the enigma that she was kept drawing me in, though I to this day have no memory at all of what we talked about during those early shampoos.

Certainly the oddity that was Bonnie soon gave way to the oddity that was her shop. She was the only operator who was ever there, and I was the only regular customer who was ever there. There were three stations, but over the months of that first summer they showed less and less evidence of ever being used.

On my sixth or seventh visit I came to understand that Bonnie must be living there, upstairs over the shop, and that she had two or three other women up there with her. They would come down sometimes, always in cheap cotton wrappers, a cigarette in one hand and a crumpled half pack in the other, to buy a Coke out of the machine in the back or to ask Bonnie for some change. Occasionally I would see a masculine shadow lounging behind one of them or a hand reach out to take the Coke that had been bought, but never did I see any of the upstairs people face to face. They simply waited in the curtained dusk of the supply room until Bonnie could attend to them.

There was, however, a swarthy, slender man—Carl, he said—whom she called her business manager and who was always cleaning the sinks or counting money at the third station. The relationship between them did not seem to be that of pimp and property, although there was no doubt in my mind by then that Bonnie was first and foremost a hooker, if not by popular demand, at least by instinct and preference.

I think it took me that long to understand because of Bonnie herself. She was clearly middle-aged. Her hair was carefully and artfully dyed, but nothing was ever going to make her body look under fifty again. I don't think it really bothered her that much anyway. Certainly by the time we parted company three years later she had let her hair go gray. It gave her face a kind of softness that matched her body's, a kind of sweet quiet or ease with herself that was contagious.

Over the months of the next fall and winter my visits became more regular, more a habit I depended on even if my hair didn't. I came; we talked; she restored my soul and called it washing my hair. Sometimes I brought her things from my kitchen, usually sweets that Grandma had made and sent her . . . for Grandma had become Bonnie's second and only other regular shampoo customer.

One of my most delightful memories of my mother, in fact, is the day she came home and, black eyes big as coat buttons, said, "Do you know that I honestly think Bonnie is . . . is not supporting herself on that shop . . ."

"Is hooking?" I offered.

"Yes! Exactly. That's what I mean. I really do!"

But I noticed the revelation of Bonnie's true calling never stopped Grandma from going twice a week for a wash and set. Even more important, I thought, was the fact that it never stopped the flow of goodies from our kitchen to Bonnie's shop.

By this time, Bonnie had become very candid about the nature of her business, and we had long conversations about the evils that attended her profession, the human damage . . . the realities, I suppose they might be called.

Bonnie was equally candid about the nature of her

relationship with Grandma and with me. She needed us. "It dresses up the shop to have you in here, and especially a nice old lady like Mrs. Alexander...makes us look legit, like a real salon," she said.

This was an explanation that I shared with Grandma. Thereafter she took an almost criminal pleasure in fulfilling her obligation to Bonnie by speaking with elaborate sweetness and impeccable propriety (she, too, had been reared middle-class, after all, and not for nothing had she learned the ways of our breed!) to the patrol officer who had begun to stroll in to the shop far too frequently for Bonnie's comfort. Nothing so animated my mother's afternoon as a disgustingly prim conversation with Officer Tolliver about the weather, politics, and the desperate state of urban crime. Her role as defender of the interesting if not the innocent was one that she was still proud of long after Bonnie had closed the shop and moved Carl back to Illinois so they could be near his children.

Bonnie's relationship with Carl was a simple one, not at all what I had at first tried to imagine for them. She had been a cook on the river—signing on to a boat going downriver to New Orleans; getting off and working awhile, as she put it. Signing on to another tug to push the barges back upriver, when she needed a rest...as she also put it. Although, she said frequently, there was little rest for a woman alone, cooking like that for an eight-man crew on a floating tin can. "Those boys!" She would shake her head in mock despair. "I swear I just loved 'em all!" Then, with great pride in herself, she would tell me, "I can still go down there to the dock right now and sign on with any captain on that river. He'd take me in a minute. Knows I'd be good to his boys. If it weren't for Carl, I'd do it, too."

Carl was her reason for being. She had made of him the surrogate life that many single folks make of their pets. Carl had worked the boats for years, and they had met there, had become friends there; but Carl had developed bad lungs. And they were getting worse. It was Carl's lungs that had driven him to Bonnie. It was Carl's lungs that had driven them both ashore. And it was Carl's lungs that were destined to take them home finally to Illinois for him to die.

"What will you do?" I asked her once, after they had decided to close the "business" and just before they left.

"Probably just live on with his boy and his wife. They've got a nice house up there, and they say I'd be welcome. I can draw Social Security off my wages from the boats in two more years. I can make it till then."

The last time I was with Bonnie, as she combed out my hair and began to dry it with the towel, she said, "You can do something for me."

It was unlike her to express her private needs or desires at all, and I understood immediately that moving inland and north was not quite as easy a thing as she had wanted me to believe. "What?"

"You can write me into one of your books someday."

"All right, I will. But why? Why would you care about that?"

"I guess I'm getting old," she said, "soft in the squash, but it would make the whole thing seem more like it's been worth it if somebody knew I'd been here."

"A lot of people know you've been here!" I was appalled by the irony of it.

"Yeah, but in all these years I guess I never did anything for Bonnie. I never had time or else I just forgot to. I wish now I had..." She stumbled. "... had built something," she said finally, "... you know, or written something like you or even had a family."

"No, you don't. You would have hated being tied down when you were younger, being rooted to a washing machine or a man."

She thought about it a minute or two while she toweled. "Yeah, I would've, wouldn't I!" She grinned at me in the mirror. Then, slyly, ducking her eyes, "Just like you would've hated my boys." She combed on a minute. "God's crazy, you know that?"

"Probably, but why'd you say so?"

"He made all the rules and then made people like me who couldn't any more keep 'em than we could fly to heaven by ourselves."

"I always sort of thought that was true of all of us."

"I reckon so," she said, totally cheerful again. "Sure is why I hanker after Him anyway."

As a confession of faith, it was as brief as it was unorthodox, but I never heard one I thought was more validated by the life and history of its confessor.

Three days later, when they were loading Carl's car with what they wanted to keep, I went by to say good-bye. As she hugged me, Bonnie said into my ear, so Carl wouldn't hear, "I guess I do make a family now with Carl and his kids, but don't forget about the book. I'd still like to be in a book."

I told her I would remember, and obviously, I have. But after all these years I don't want to leave it just as a promise kept. I want to say here, as I never could then, that Bonnie did build something even if she didn't know it and I wasn't generous enough to tell her so. I want to say that only in Bonnie and in one very simple country priest have I ever found the unencumbered humility that would let me or any other spiritual stray rest effortlessly in its faith.

So, Bonnie, forgive me, if you are reading this. I have kept my promise, but the book I have put you in is not about you after all. It's about grace and about how I would to God that I had more of yours.

THE
TRANSFIGURATION

O F ALL THE HOLY DAYS IN ORDINARY TIME AND of all the mysteries celebrated in the season, the Transfiguration suffers the greatest degree of popular indifference. Ironically, it also enjoys the greatest degree of popular acceptance.

So far as I know, no major (or even minor) branch of Christianity denies the Transfiguration. The event itself was recorded by three independent witnesses; moreover, according to the propers for the day, the event also had a historical precedent in the radiant transfiguration of Moses as he descended Sinai. (So great was that radiance, in fact, that the children of Israel feared to even come near Moses, again according to the propers.)

The denial of a transfiguration has never, therefore, been a problem. Nor has there ever been any significant question about the accuracy of the accounts, about the fact that what the Apostles said they saw really was what they saw and/or that what they saw really was what happened. Probably no other miracle in the Bible can make that claim—has ever been questioned so little or analyzed so infrequently for credibility, in other words.

It happened—There it is—So what? has, instead,

---

*Date in Roman and Anglican calendar; some denominations now observe the Transfiguration before Lent.

been the attitude. According to three grown men, two historic figures moved back and forth through time both in their comings and goings and in the prophecies of their conversation, and our reaction to this bit of news is intellectual acceptance without wonder!

It is as if the mind boggles and ceases to function in the face of so vast a possibility. Certainly mine does. Like the church, I don't question...never have questioned, in fact...the Transfiguration. I simply walk around it and go through the motions of it because I don't know what else to do with it...how to grasp it; how to incorporate it; how to employ it. It lies beyond both my intellect and my faith; and without one or the other, it lies beyond me. I am thereby robbed of rejoicing.

But if I cannot yet incorporate the Transfiguration, cannot yet rejoice in it, I can now, in my middle years, at least reverence its reality. Even that is progress. It is also the result of having shared space and time with Lawrence.

5.

JUST A LITTLE ABOUT LAWRENCE

WE HAVE A PRESENCE AT OUR HOUSE. EVEN after all these years, Sam still does not like for me to broadcast the fact, so I don't make my statement casually or without reason.

His name is Lawrence, and he has been with us for twenty-five years and two houses. When Nora was seven, Mary five, Laura two, and before John, Wade, Sam, Jr., and Rebecca even were, we bought a house in the city. It was one of those circa 1900 houses that are always found in center cities nowadays. Originally a middle-class triumph, it and all the other houses around it had done a slow slide into disrepute. The surrounding houses had been refurbished and were ready to be recycled, this time into middle-class triumphs of inner-city restoration. Only this house stood between the neighborhood and possible perfection.

With three young children, a college teaching appointment, and a doctor-husband returning to school for a fellowship in pulmonary medicine, I somehow could muster almost no enthusiasm for house restoration, much less whole neighborhoods of it. A quick rundown of family finances, however, militated for the present, dilapidated choice. The house we had been renting was to be condemned for an interstate exchange, a fate I thought was eminently appropriate

considering the eccentricities of both its plumbing
and its heating. It was not that I hated being evicted,
but that I despaired of what we were being evicted
to. Nonetheless, as Sam so succinctly put it, this
house was all there was. Take it or leave it.

We made an offer on the house... one slightly in
excess of insanity and even more in excess of what
we could afford. Obviously Sam had decided that he
was going to solve the fixing-up problem by leaving
us no money at all with which to "fix up." It was at
least one way to get out of the work for which neither
of us had time or energy. So he made his offer, I held
my breath, and the realtor laughed out loud. The
owner would never take it... no way ever! She already had refused three offers that were considerably
higher. The last one had been only four thousand
dollars more, granted, but it had been from her
bishop himself who had wanted to put a boys' home
there. The realtor elaborated in detail what a major
decision it had been for her; and since, devout
Roman Catholic that her late husband had been and
that she still was, she had not succumbed to the pull
of church and clergy, he felt it very unlikely that she
would succumb to us in our evicted state of need.
Sam shrugged... I remember the gesture well... and
said it was the best we could do; ask her.

That night, sitting morosely in our about-to-be-
demolished kitchen, we got a phone call. It was the
owner herself calling to say that she had received our
offer and was accepting it. Never one to dally with
the niceties, I heard myself responding with a simple
"Why?" To which she responded, "Because Lawrence
told me to. He wants children in the house." It never
occurred to me to ask her who Lawrence was. In

fact, so great was my state of shock, I didn't even
question what she had said until days later.

So we moved—bags, baggage, and babies—into a
house that had been empty for several years and that
was more than casually distressed in all its seams and
crevices. We cleaned and ripped out and made do as
best we could, for there truly was no slush fund for
repairs and restoration. Over the weeks that followed
we met all the neighbors... warm, energetic folk
with whom we were to share the next sixteen years
and—naturally, was there ever any question?—the
restoration of the neighborhood. Yet none of them
was named Lawrence.

Once we were settled, or as settled as we were
going to get without any money, I became friends
with the former owner just by sheer contact and
numerous phone calls about how we made what work
and when. Finally one day during the Christmas
holidays after we had moved in in the fall, I asked
the question: "Who is Lawrence?"

She laughed the most cascading, musical laughter
I think I can ever remember having heard. It was
crystal and happy and almost angelic, so much so
that it startled me, for Rose, much as I liked her, was
neither crystalline nor cascading. Lawrence had been
her husband. He had died in the upstairs front
bedroom. He was still there. Hadn't we seen him
yet? He was very happy that we had come... had, in
fact, been the reason she hadn't sold to the other
bidders. Lawrence was very opinionated about people, even in this life, and he had become more so in
his new one. We'd see him soon, and she really had
to go.

Sam listened to my recitation of our conversation

and then shook his head. "Crazy," he said, a position from which he has moved only grudgingly and with deliberation over the years since then. He threw in an addendum. "Doesn't the Roman church allow some of this angel and ghost stuff into its credo?"...we were very young, you see; very young...and we had not yet overtly met Lawrence.

It was not long, however, before we began to understand Lawrence. Mary, age five and chubby with a kind of Mediterranean beauty that took your breath away, was sleeping in Lawrence's bedroom. She had chosen it as hers before Rose's explanations, and she had no intention of leaving it now. She thought a ghost was "a pretty neat thing" and a dead man's bedroom was "even neater," to quote her. (She was young also, a child of our own infancy.)

Then came the spring and Mary's complaints that Laura was pulling the covers off her bed during the night.

"I don't think that Laura can get out of her crib," I insisted.

"Then it's Nora," Mary countered. "Somebody is yanking my covers off and waking me up!"

"Have you ever seen either of them in your room?"

No, she was always sound asleep when her "bratty sisters"... that's a direct quote also... came in. Finally, after numerous mornings of complaint and equally insistent denial on the part of the two accused, I suggested to her that we secretly set her clock for three-thirty, since four o'clock seemed to be the hour of her harassment. Maybe, if she could wake up in time, she could catch the culprit redhanded. She thought it was a marvelous idea... also neat, I believe . . . and I set the clock for her. Nothing happened.

"You told them I was going to try to catch them!" she accused.

"No," I said, telling the truth. "No one knows we set your clock."

We tried again. Nothing. By the fourth night she was getting bored with the game and also cross from interrupted sleep. I suggested that we give it up, but she was adamant. She was going to keep on until she caught one or the other of them. As I looked at her sleep-deprived eyes, it occurred to me for the first time to wonder why the errant sister, whichever one she was, did not look equally haggard. Surely if nighttime pranks could weary one child, they should weary another equally as much. Curious.

Then on the fifth night, Mary came bursting into our bedroom without knocking, a strictly forbidden violation of house rules. "Mother! Mother!" She was inarticulate. I had to see right now. I staggered into her bedroom . . . after three babies, Sam had learned to sleep through anything . . . and there was her bed, disheveled and with the covers torn loose at the foot.

"He opened my door and came in! I saw him! He's doing it! Look!" And as I looked, her rocking chair began to rock merrily. Then it stopped just as abruptly. "Isn't it wonderful!" She was ecstatic.

Poltergeist? I didn't think so. It was much too benign, and the rocking of the chair had been jolly, good-humored, almost avuncular. I decided to say nothing. Children, unfortunately, have no such sense of decorum. The breakfast table was abuzz next morning with ghosts and nocturnal miracles, to which Sam contributed a withering "Humbug!" for the children

and an "I want a word with you" to me. The drift of
his thinking was that we were in no way going to
encourage this kind of thing. It was patently impossible and not at all funny. He had spoken. Having no
answer, I beat a discreet retreat from the field of
battle.

Lawrence, however, did not see it that way. He
continued to wake Mary, but she became adept at
going back to sleep. Also, as the weather grew
warmer, the air on her feet became less of a chilling
shock, and she managed to sleep soundly through
the summer months.

Then the other girls began to see Lawrence in the
hall, a phenomenon that both Sam and I credited to
active imaginations and to a certain amount of jealou-
sy of Mary's honored role as harassee of choice. That
is, I did until I saw him. He crossed the hall one
afternoon from the bedroom toward the upstairs
front bath just as I was mounting the back stairs. He
had on a darkish overcoat with the collar pulled up
counterspy-style and a brimmed hat pulled down so
that I could see none of his face. I could also see
through him to the wallpaper pattern beyond, an
unexpected attribution that I found to be rather
disconcerting.

Having heard well my husband's admonitions and
having agreed (whether he would believe that or not)
with his position that enough foolishness was enough,
I had not engaged the girls in any detailed conversations about Lawrence since the spring. That afternoon, however, I broke the silence. "Nora, what
does Lawrence look like?"

"I don't know. You can't ever see his face. He's got

this hat on all the time, pulled down like. And some kind of overcoatlike thing with the collar up."

"Can you see through him?"

"Oh, Mama! Of course you can! You don't think he's really there, do you?"

I felt suddenly cold inside and, at the same time, intellectually piqued by the contradiction in my child's statement. "Then where is he?"

"How would I know? He just likes us and likes to play with us."

I left it alone, but I never forgot it.

In the dining room of the house there was a most remarkable chandelier. It was so remarkable that my father, a very godly man of much learning and most gentlemanly ways, when he first walked into the dining room, looked it squarely in the face and said quietly, "That's the most god-abandoned thing I've ever seen!" It was the only time in my whole life I heard him use that expression.

Even Sam finally concluded that the chandelier had to go. We would just have to find some way to scrape up the money for a replacement or else patch the ceiling, but that forest of glassy pretension and cankered brass was simply not going to hang over another Sunday dinner. The kids, however, raised a veritable howl of protest. Didn't we know that that was where Lawrence now slept at night?

Even if I had not heard this one . . . and Sam was certainly not in any frame of mind to be told it . . . Granddaddy was determined. He would buy us a new light fixture as a gift, and Lawrence could take the hindmost. The protests degenerated into tears and then into genuine anxiety. Finally both men compromised. The old chandelier would be taken

down, but it would be put up in the attic instead of
out on the trash bins. Realizing it was the best they
were going to get, the girls settled; and our second
fall progressed into our second winter. Lawrence
continued to enter into their conversations from time
to time, but life took up routine and therefore pattern, in which he, being merely a part, was less
particular and less noticeable.

Over the years we were joined by John, then
Wade, then Sam, Jr., and finally Rebecca. We had
long since restored the old house in midtown and
modernized it, but even that was never going to
make it large enough to hold us all comfortably.
Granddaddy had died, and Grandma had come to
live with us. It was just all too much. Moreover,
Daddy yearned for the country. His practice was
established. There were partners to share the night
call. I had, years before, given up teaching for writ-
ing, a profession better practiced in isolation than in
community. The country was ideal from my point of
view. The decision was made. We would leave the
city and move as soon as we could.

Rebecca was two and immune to all the fuss of
looking for a farm to buy, of finding a realtor who
would fool with our multiplicities and clutter, and—
most dreadful of all—of looking for a buyer, but the
rest of us were in agony. With the restoration of the
house and of the neighborhood, property values had
shot way up; so had our rather sizable cash invest-
ment in materials, repairs, and two additions. Consequently, not a lot of folks were both able to afford the
house and young enough to want to take on what was
always going to be "an older home."

Meanwhile we had found the farm...just absolutely

perfect. The kids loved it; Sam was radiant; and I was filled with a peace I have continued to feel ever since that first day when we walked on the place and I knew I was home at last. It was right for us. If we could only sell that house! What we had once loved and been happy in became an albatross, a burden we couldn't unload.

It seemed to us that hundreds of people came through, looked, and left. Bet Brown, our realtor, was in despair after three months. She complained bitterly to me one afternoon that if she had to climb those attic stairs one more time, she thought she'd kill the client right there on the landing and wash her hands of the whole deal!

So it went, until the late spring day when the doorbell rang and I opened it to a middle-aged man. I looked at him, and a voice in my head said, "This is it!" And sure enough, it was. His realtor followed docilely behind him, but there was never any question that this was our buyer. We were tearful we were so relieved. To the country we were going!

Three days later Bet brought the papers for us to sign. The older children watched fascinated as their father and I signed the copies that would relieve us of the house and make the farm possible. We stayed up late afterward and celebrated. What a happy festival we made there in the old kitchen's dim light! Then to bed and to a deep, heavy sleep. After so much anxiety for so long, it was the sweetest rest I could ever remember—until about four o'clock.

Suddenly there was the most alarming noise in the bathroom followed by Mary's hollering followed by a huge crash downstairs in the kitchen followed by the attic door's flying open. Even Sam woke up for this one. Mary was standing in the middle of the hall, eighteen and as indignant as she could be. "Lawrence just pulled my toes!" She was livid, so livid her father didn't bother to argue with her.

The hall floor was covered with dirty clothes that had obviously been dragged out of the built-in clothes hamper in the front bathroom. Picking them up, I headed to the bathroom to put them back into the hamper... what hamper? The thing had been ripped literally out of the wall, the wooden door splintered and left wounded and useless in the floor of the bathroom. Sam glowered, but to his eternal credit let it be said that he never challenged the actuality of what we were looking at.

The attic door was plainly open, and he rebolted it as he turned back down the hall and headed for the kitchen, followed by the six Tickles who were big enough to have been awakened by the ruckus. The kitchen was a mess. The notes and bills and lists that had been magnetized to the refrigerator were strewn all over the floor. The freezer door was open, and the food had been spilled.

"Lawrence is mad. He just doesn't want us to leave." She was too big to paddle, but I think that was the only thing that saved her, for Sam turned on Mary in a whirl. "Don't you ever say that again!"

She looked him straight in the eye. "But it's true," and she went about cleaning up.

Back upstairs I said to him "Why?" and with much less sureness than he had shown downstairs, he answered me, "I don't know."

We moved uneventfully... uneventful as most moves go, that is. On the next to the last load, Laura said to her father that he had better go to the attic and get

the chandelier. He was aghast. Why would we take
that old thing? "You'd just better," she said. "It's
where Lawrence still sleeps."

Sam absolutely refused until John, age seven, announced he wouldn't move unless the chandelier
went. Defeated and/or politic in his choice of what
ground to defend, Sam mounted the attic steps one
last time to retrieve the chandelier. It was gone. The
children didn't believe him, and there was a mass
exodus up the rickety stairs to confirm the fact that
he had not pulled a fast one. It was indeed gone.
Even I went up just to be sure. John was cross, and
Sam, Jr., cried because Lawrence would have no
place to sleep on the farm. Both accused Sam of
having thrown the thing away. Even gentle Laura
was suspicious of her father until his protestations
convinced us that he simply hadn't even remembered the chandelier, much less thought enough
about it to bother with disposing of it.

That afternoon Bet came by with the last of the
warranties and the keys for the farmhouse. John
immediately interrupted her errand with the tale of
our lost chandelier. "No, honey," she reassured him,
"it's up there behind the eaves and beyond the
landing. I saw it week before last when I was up
there for the last time."

He stoutly defended himself, and I assured her the
thing was really gone. "Nonsense. Come on. I'll
show you!" And Bet, who hated those stairs with
fervor, was on her way.

In a few minutes she was back. "It's gone!" Her
voice had a kind of hollow sound to it.

"I told you," said John.

"But it really was there when I made my last check of everything before we closed!"

"I know," I said. I had given up.

So, happy, but a bit less cheerful than we might otherwise have been, we moved without Lawrence and his chandelier, the last load being only us, the children, and the dog. We moved in June, put in a partial crop and started a herd that summer, and settled contentedly into remembered patterns of earlier years and earlier ways. Life was good. Mary went off to college for her first year. Nora and her husband had a baby boy, which did wonders for all of us. And I got up grateful every morning—consciously grateful—for where I was and who I was. No one thought of our situation as being life without Lawrence. He was never mentioned anymore.

Then one sunny morning in October the phone rang, and it was Bet Brown. "I have your ghost."

"What?"

"We have Lawrence . . . or I think we must. Someone keeps turning on the lights in the middle of the night. And this past week the TV in the den has been coming on about four o'clock every morning, blaring away until someone goes down and turns it off. Then last night it started with the radios. My husband says I have to do something."

"Do you have an attic?"

"Yeah, but the chandelier's not up there. My son already looked. It's like Lawrence is mad at me for selling the house."

I tried to be jovial. "I'm glad it's you and not me with this problem."

"Honestly," she snorted back at me. "I don't even

believe in ghosts. But he really is doing this stuff. . . I mean that really is why it's happening, isn't it?"

"I suspect so." I was struggling to be as detached as possible.

"Well, honestly!" And she hung up.

Two weeks later she called again. "Haven't you got any idea about what to do with this thing?"

"None."

"It's wearing us out! No one can sleep."

"I really am sorry, Bet." I could tell from the silence that she didn't believe me. "The only time we ever had trouble was the night we signed the papers and he went berserk. I honestly think it will get better all by itself." Then I added, "And I really do wish he'd come home," and realized I meant it.

"I just wish he'd *go* home!" Bet said and hung up emphatically.

Six weeks later just at Christmas when the weather was still crisp but not yet bitter, Laura came sweetly into the kitchen just at supper. "Guess who's in the side yard outside my window?"

No one should be! We were miles out in the country! "Who?" I asked in alarm.

"Lawrence!" She was plainly overjoyed.

"Are you sure?"

"Of course I'm sure!" And she was, too, because he was.

Within ten days John had seen him in the den, and I, looking down the steps one afternoon, had seen him in the lower hall. He turned and looked directly at me for the first time in all those years, and we made a kind of silent pact. He was home to stay. He may not like the country too well, but he likes us well enough to hang in there.

And so it has been in all the years since then. He comes and goes. The children and now the grandson speak of him as familiarly as they speak of one another.

Sam is still skittish of too much talk. More now than in our city years. I think he fears that we may all misunderstand what is happening... that in too ready a familiarity with whatever Lawrence is we may accept cheap or romantic explanations for him.

We are no longer young, nor are the children of our youth any longer young, either. We know more now, all of us, and we know enough to understand Sam's hesitancy about the easy explanations.

So I am not recording all these events casually or without reason. I am recording them because they are part of us certainly, part of the myth that is this one particular family. And partly because, being the only rift in time I have ever known personally, Lawrence has given me a lot more than Sam's doubt or the children's delight. He has taught me about myself.

You see, there are times when I don't even believe in Lawrence, and that scares me because I can remember other times, like that first time on the back stairs, when I believed in him most earnestly.

There are other times when I believe in Lawrence as an invention that has given the children and me, if not their father, great amusement and that has bonded us in a way that only myths can. I can remember all the Christmases, for instance, when someone would put a gift under the tree and sign the card, "From Lawrence," and we all knew it was a hoax even if we couldn't determine the hoaxer. But I also know that the fractured clothes hamper and Bet

Brown's part of our story are absolutely true, and she will be the first to swear to it, believe me.

There are other times when I believe in the projection of Lawrence. We were burglarized here once. An odd crime for the country. We thought of it more in the city, but it happened here. (And, indeed, almost happened again within a month of our first experience.) It would be hard to explain to anyone who has never known that crime exactly how pervasive are its consequences, especially for young children whose rooms have been destroyed and whose toys have been removed. There is no doubt that, when Bet Brown's second call came, five weeks after our burglary and three weeks after our burglar's second attempt at us, the intensity of my response, of my wishing deeply that Lawrence would come home to us, was born of an even more intense and instantaneous realization that there would be no more burglaries if he were to. And that, too, is a hard statement to confess publicly.

So what Lawrence has given me is the liberating proof that I am out of my depth, that I am inconsistent, that I don't know how to use things that I both see and sometimes don't see. And that somehow it is all right to live not knowing how, but just using each day's particular version of things as being that day's particular truth. Certainly that part of living with Lawrence is part of me tonight as we are getting ready for evening prayer and the Feast of the Transfiguration.

ST. MARY THE VIRGIN

THIS DAY, ONE OF THE MOST ANCIENT OF HOLY days, has only in fairly recent times come to enjoy such an elaborate title. It was, and still is in most places, just Mary Day; and the more Protestant the congregation or denomination, the greater the tendency to ignore it, especially in this country.

Like many other shifts in our time, the return to some acknowledgment of Mary Day, even under the burden of its full and official title, interests me, promises me something I want. It seems to foreshadow a time when many of the differences that have shamed us as a religion will soften into understandable variations of perception, into the less intense distance of ecclesiastical history. For that reason Mary Day is particularly dear to my mind and my hoping.

But Mary Day is far more intimately wound into my understanding of woman and of having been woman all the years of my life. The fact that we can make of the Virgin—and have—any symbol or justification we want to for the ways and purposes of the female half of the human race probably explains the way that we have fought so viciously among ourselves over her meaning. There have even been times when I have contended that perhaps one of the greatest of the Virgin's contributions has been this using of her as symbol, icon, battling ground, when the faith has had to explore new eras, new sites, and new converts. Certainly for me privately she has been so, and I hope someday to thank her, if not here then hereafter.

6.

THE LADIES
REMEMBERING

I AM NOT A FANCIER OF FLOWERS, AT LEAST not in the usual sense of that phrase. But I do have a rather considerable fondness for geraniums, probably due more to their acrid odor and vibrant color than to the fact that they are flowers.

Women learn early that anything that is alive is a potential and probable responsibility. As a result we become very selective about which flora and fauna to accept, and we become very analytical about our own selection processes. Thus my relative sureness that the odor in particular matters. For that smell I would water and prune anything every day for the rest of my life.

Geraniums happily have yet another virtue that also endears them to me . . . they attract everything, and their pots become a display every summer of life on a miniature scale. The first year we came to the farm to live, I confess I bought geraniums at the feed store to try to give some liveliness to our front porch. That structure, which faces southeast into the early morning heat, suffers from the impoverishment of size and grace that often characterizes southern houses and that leads to the wondrous piece of vocabulary, "the stoop." I never have quite known whether the house was supposed to stoop to meet the inelegance of its entryway or whether the whole was so compro-

mised by the roofless blob of poured concrete as to
make its owner want to stoop. Whichever the way of
the thing, we have a stoop just big enough to accommodate two small stands and two pots of geraniums.

Warmed by the morning sun and kept breathlessly
toasty by the brick and concrete around them, the
geraniums of our first year flourished with uncontrol-
lable abandon, and I became quite attached to their
courage and their good humor. The children likewise
shared my sense of pleasure in the heartiness of the
flowers. With the coming of fall we were so bonded
to the pots of color as to be unwilling to give them
over to their demise. Sam set one pot in the garage
window to take the winter sun in a more secluded
and sheltered environment. The other he set on a
contrived ledge in the kitchen window to appease
the children and me.

The window, like most kitchen ones, sits dead
center of a double sink and looks out over the
backyard and the lower pastures toward the pond.
Doing dishes isn't my favorite chore, but the view
from the window is one of my choice pleasures. As a
result I have always managed to dawdle over the
dishes in the best of times. The addition of the
geranium pot that first October further slowed the
washing-up process.

For the first week or two, the geranium was as
lush inside as it had been out on the stoop. By the
first of November, of course, it was beginning to
show withdrawal symptoms, and its leaves were less
thick, its blooms less vivid. Sam fertilized both pots
and waited.

A week later, the weather already chilly and the
view turning gray into the winter vista, I was washing

the pots and loading the dishwasher when I had an overwhelming sense of someone or something staring at me. The sensation was not eerie or unpleasant, just persistent. I shook it off and closed down the kitchen for the evening.

The next morning I was drawing water for the teakettle when the same sense of presence overcame me. I shortened my sights this time (it was the cold light of day now) and looked at the geranium. Sitting placidly on the edge of the pot was a baby frog. Only his throat was moving, but he was studying me with all the sobriety and intensity of a Martian on his first trip to earth. The obvious superiority of his stance was disconcerting, but his presence was charming. I made a move toward him, and he was as quickly gone back into the pot. I called Sam and the children to come and see, but nowhere could we detect any evidence of a frog. In fact, Sam teased me by explaining to the children that I was, as they all knew, a perpetual dreamer and romantic. In part, I think, he believed his own story.

The day ended as all days do, and once more I closed down the kitchen without incident. The frog was forgotten by everyone except me. I went up to read in bed, leaving Sam to work as he does each night on the kitchen table with his medical records and reading. About midnight he came upstairs laughing and insisting that I wake up. Above his poking and chuckling, I could distinctly hear downstairs the croaking of a frog. "Nearly scared me to death the first time!" was Sam's comment as I got up to go and see. And there on the rim of the pot sat our visitor, for all the world looking as if he owned the place.

The next morning the frog came up to the rim

from under the leaves as soon as I turned on the kitchen lights. By breakfast the children had agreed to name him Jeremiah since that was during the years that the song beginning, "Jeremiah was a bull-frog," was popular. And Jeremiah was admitted to our lives as a permanent resident. He gave up his visitor status with some reluctance, I thought, for it cost him his superior position among us. But in time he became as truculent and rewarding as any other family member.

The children and I could not for the life of us figure out what Jeremiah was eating, but he definite-ly was growing to rather impressive proportions. By December he had become a full-size frog with a deep throttling kind of croak. He was silent as a church mouse as long as someone was in the kitchen with him. The minute, however, that everyone left the kitchen, Jeremiah raised his protest with all the ferocity of a nine-month-old baby put down for a nap. Even the lights did not fool him. He wanted human companionship at all times, period. Eventually we simply learned to sleep in spite of the croaking; and Jeremiah, like a bright child, got smart enough to give up his nighttime protest, restricting his de-mands to those for daytime company. That was easier for us to accommodate, and we fell into a comfortable arrangement of living together.

As he grew older, Jeremiah gained a certain fastidiousness that the children thought humorous and that I found somewhat less appealing. Every morning when I came into the kitchen to begin breakfast, Jeremiah arose from his geranium bed, hopped to the rim of the pot, turned around with his face to the center, and defecated onto the kitchen

windowsill. That chore accomplished for the day, he
turned around to face out and watched me studiously
as I cleaned up the mess he had just made. It was an
interesting way to begin the day.

As a present and in an attempt to encourage such
exquisite concern for cleanliness, Sam gave Jeremiah
a bathtub of his own for Christmas. The children
were mystified as Daddy emptied one of those sam-
ple pill bottles that doctors get by the hundreds, cut
it into halves lengthwise, sealed the semicircular neck
with bathtub caulk, and then set the whole in
Jeremiah's pot. The minute Sam filled the contriv-
ance with water, it was clear that Jeremiah at least
was not mystified by the gift; and thereafter he
added an extended bath to his morning routine.

It was, in fact, the bathtub that also solved the
mystery of Jeremiah's increasing corpulence. One
morning Jeremiah seemed hesitant to jump into his
swimming pool. He sat looking pointedly at it, but
he would not get in. Curious, I lifted a geranium leaf
to investigate and found only a bit of trash in the
water. I lifted it out and discovered to my surprise
that it was a bit of raw hamburger that had inadvertently
made its way into the tub. The question of Jeremiah's
diet was resolved, and I was reasonably sure I could
guess at his supplier.

Late that night as I lay reading in bed, I heard the
refrigerator door open. Slipping downstairs quietly, I
watched as Sam set at least a dozen tiny dots of raw
meat carefully into the pot. "I thought so," I said
from the kitchen doorway, and he at least had the
grace to blush.

By mid-January Jeremiah was beginning to feel his
oats. He took to jumping out of the pot for little side

trips around the sink. We would find him looking at us from the watering pot or sitting on top of the kitchen matches. Then came the inevitable day when he discovered the joys of jumping, not to mention the joys of being good at it. He leapt from the sill to the stove, narrowly missing a pot of simmering beans.

Sam called a family conference. If we kept Jeremiah, we obviously stood a chance of losing him to an unattractive death by boiling or frying. If we let him out to the elements, we stood a chance of his death by inability to survive what he had never known in more clement times. The children voted to take their chances inside. By now the thought of losing him was as painful to them as to us. So, many a time during February and March someone had to grab a frog in midcareen. We became rather proficient at it actually, and I still think Jeremiah may be the reason John is so adept now as a catcher. Early training can do a lot for a child.

But then April came. The light grew brighter and the days longer. The geranium began to bud and Jeremiah to decline. Hormones had obviously got him. He bellowed with a new and mournful call, like a foghorn with a chest cold. He refused to come out to the countertops and eventually to come to the rim. When for three days he refused even his good housekeeping practices, we knew it was time to face the facts of due process.

Sam and Rebecca took the geranium out and set it in the grass at the base of the front steps. For days Rebecca went faithfully every day to water the flower and the frog, and to talk to Jeremiah. For days he was there every time she went. Then there came the afternoon when he was not in the pot. She was dejected, but her despair evaporated when the frog reappeared in the pot by evening. And so it went for three or four weeks, Jeremiah gone during the days but home to sleep.

Just as I had decided that we might indeed keep him, there came the dusk when he did not return to his pot. For four or five days Rebecca watered and hoped, but Jeremiah was gone . . . until she found him living in the flowerbed surrounded by a veritable tribe of frogs. There was no question that it was Jeremiah, however, and she was content somehow to release him to his own. They spent the summer together, she and Jeremiah, having conversations across the porch railing about how things were in the flowerpot, but Jeremiah was no longer a part of our lives at any intimate level.

And in the years since then, the geraniums have continued to house a variety of creatures. One summer it was a ferociously beautiful war spider whose egg sack was the size of a small apple by the time winter came. Last year it was a kitten with an uncanny fondness for the warm pot and the pungent odor of the bruised stems. This summer we are housing a swallow family. The mother, gliderlike and glossy dark in her swoops around the porch, has completely filled the area under the leaves with her nest and has closed the whole thing over at the top to the most narrow opening possible. I always check to see whether or not she's home before I water the plant, but sometimes it's impossible to detect her through the narrow opening. Yesterday I miscalculated and watered while she was home, causing her enormous agitation. This morning she is back in her pot, apparently having decided to forgive me my error.

She will be gone soon, of course, just as Jeremiah, the kitten, the war spider, and all the others before her have gone. In fact, her babies and her mate have long since flown off to new quarters of their own, and she will follow them when the weather turns. We shall miss her, especially when the boys throw her nest away before they bring the geranium in to winter. But for right now, during these dry, heavy days of August, her gloss and the flowers' waxy red brighten the stoop and give a lilt to my morning steps. They each make me admit once again that nurturing what lives is womanness for me—the work and the joy being each other and the same always.

All of which matters not at all in the great scheme of things probably, except that today, August 16, is the first day of a new school year for the children, and yesterday was, naturally enough, August 15, the Feast of St. Mary the Virgin. I didn't go to church, of course. We don't mark the day very rigorously in America, and thus there was no service to go to.

But today, in the blessed quiet of our abandonment, the geranium, the swallow, and I thought to mark the holy day, somewhat belatedly, in our own way, by being ladies together and by remembering all the life that has stopped awhile and then passed on through us. Speaking for all the ladies, I think I can safely say that we are grateful.

HOLY CROSS DAY

For centuries the celebration of the central symbol of our faith got caught up in the fuss over whether or not the real cross and its wood still existed and, if so, where. Most of us now are content to say that the answers to that dilemma are yes and everywhere. In the same way that the risen Lord exists in the bread and wine, so does His cross exist among us in all its holy uses. The eyes of conversion, looking, see. Thus it has always been and will be always.

But that ready solution was arrived at only with great difficulty and only after some false starts. Originally observed in September, Holy Cross Day was moved, at one time in papal history, to May to become a spring festival and to extend, by means of a concrete symbol, Easter's hold on the faithful.

In due time reversing its position, the Roman church returned the day to Trinity and to its original place on the fourteenth of September. In more recent times and for reasons I have never been privy to, other denominations like Lutheranism and Episcopalianism that had never observed Holy Cross at all suddenly began to add the festival to their liturgical calendars.

Whatever ecclesiastical gossip there may be behind such revisions and decisions, the reason for

Holy Cross as a major feast day is very clear. Malachi Martin, the Christian writer and theologian, having made many brilliant and substantial observations, has also made a very simple one that cuts more deeply than all the rest and that appertains directly here. Martin says that we tend to see Christ as a hero; a great man in history; one comparable to Abe Lincoln or Gandhi—one worthy of inclusion in Western Civilization 101–102, in other words.

Of all the places one could file the Son of God, Western Civilization 101–102 is probably the safest, the one most likely to demythologize Him right down to Mahatma's battles or Ole Abe's level of honesty. The trouble seems to be, however, that while our intentions may be able to wedge the Christ—literally as well as metaphorically—into a college syllabus on great human beings, even the bravest of us can't quite shove His cross in after Him.

It doesn't fit very well, apparently because it stayed after He ascended. Call that cross whatever you will—amulet, icon, relic, symbol—it still hangs around our necks and on our walls, marks our mercy as well as our worship, sanctifies our holy places, and in corruptions of its form salutes the dark ones. Everywhere visible, it will do all things, in fact, except be domesticated by our culture.

7.

FROM THESE THINGS

For me it happened with my dressing table. It seems so simple now, but it was both frightening and very disconcerting at the time.

Rebecca had started school at last. For the first time in twenty-five years, I was at home alone for part of the day, free to play without interruption for five delicious hours among my pots and pans, my closets and linens, my books and files. Always before, when I would begin to straighten and organize, clean out, throw away, decorate, Sam would say, "You're nesting again!" and I would realize abruptly and with joy that he was right. I was late—had been late for two or three weeks, sometimes a month.

With us the ordering of life always announced the beginning of life as well. Or, to put it the other way around, new life always presented itself at our house by ordering the old one we already had. It was always somewhere between a joke and an irony for me that it was a medical household in which such a nonmedical system worked; but Sam always shrugged it off with nonchalance, his step lighter and his grin bigger each time he was right.

So the sorting of toys and the storing of clothes, the cataloging of books and the tossing of old dishes were always followed without comment or remark after that by the changing of the kindergartener to a

bed, the toddler to a junior bed, the baby to a
trundle, and the crib to a new bumper pad and a
fresh mattress cover. Each new Tickle arrived to
clean closets, scrubbed shelves, and organized draw-
ers, none of which mattered a whit to him or her.
But everyone else was terribly grateful since, for at
least eighteen more months, it was most unlikely
that I would feel the urge to sort us out again.

But this time it was different. Sam cocked his head
when he saw the new scarf go on, but he didn't say
anything. Actually I didn't say anything either, because I didn't know what to say. In fact, I wanted to
say something, something like "What's happening to
me?" but that seemed like a silly, almost melodra-
matic way to start a conversation about a dresser
scarf. It wasn't the scarf anyway; it was my compulsion to get it that I wanted to talk about and couldn't.

It was one of those sunny days of early fall when
my obsession was born. Rebecca had been in kinder-
garten more than a month, but I had already discovered
the luxury of buying groceries alone—and in the
daylight! From that discovery it had been a quick hop
to discovering that I could buy cosmetics and bath
supplies somewhere besides the grocery store, and
also in the daylight. I was, in fact, buying hand lotion
and cold cream when I thought suddenly to myself,
I can have them both out on a dresser now!

It was an easy progression from there to realizing
that I could move the bedroom lowboy under the
mirror near the bed and have a dresser again! A
place of my own. Not a room, mind you, but a little
place, a kind of shrine to my memory of how those
adult women of my childhood had looked and smelled
and honored themselves.

I put the hand lotion down and abandoned the cold cream without ever even picking it up. I didn't want those functional bottles and ordinary brands. I didn't know what I did want, but I knew I would recognize it when I saw it... and I knew that I had to have the scarf first.

For almost three weeks after I had moved the lowboy into place under the mirror, I tried to find a scarf for it. I went through every catalog we had on hand. (In the country, the catalog is still the store of choice, even for finery like dresser scarves.) When that didn't work, I went into the city one day and wandered through two department stores, but nothing drew me to it, mainly I think because I was so self-absorbed with trying to figure out why I was doing this. Why everything else in my life was totally arrested until I could find a dresser scarf.

Then one day, just before the Thanksgiving holidays began, I found it. It was in my linen closet, folded away in the horde of leftovers that I had packed away there when Mrs. Tickle and later my own mother had broken up housekeeping. It was the simplest piece of hemmed cotton, very plain but very soft from myriad washings. In its plainness it was perfect, and I gave a little squeeze of thanks to whichever grandmother or aunt or cousin had made it.

Once back in the bedroom, I was horrified to realize that my fingers were shaking, so great was my need to get the scarf in place before the school bus could bring me an audience. And it was just that! I didn't want the children to see me doing this thing, sanctifying this place. I didn't want to share it with them either, this sense of having made from memory and self a thing, an object, a concrete geography. Not

yet. Later, when I was surer perhaps, but not now.
So Sam only cocked his head, and I, escaping
unchallenged, was left both anxious for, and afraid of,
their questions.

Because I really was out of lotion and cleansing
cream, I had to make the next move before the
holidays could overtake me. More settled this time,
more sure that whatever this was about was all right,
I drove back to the city and walked the cosmetic
counters. Since I almost never use cosmetics and
then badly, I didn't have to waste time on testing
them. I only had to look at them, knowing absolutely
that the right color and shape would make themselves known.

Sure enough, there for more money than I had
ever spent in my entire life for cosmetics sat a most
substantial set of glazed jars with gold letters and
handsome aquamarine lids of just the correct ful-
someness and excellence. Without batting an eye, I
said to the consultant behind the counter, "Do you
have hand lotion and cold cream in this line?" She
did, and I didn't even ask the prices. The bottles
were perfect in their square dimensions with their
rounded corners and their incised lettering.

Once back at home, my hands shook again. They
should have been moved by the enormity of the
price I had just paid out of a budget full of children
to feed and educate. But the shaking was perfuncto-
ry, and I knew it. It was born more of excitement
than guilt, and I knew that, too. Something very
right was happening here, and whatever it was, it
pleased me with its sense of serious health, not
waste... *of merging*, I thought, *into things*.

Because I got away with the scarf and the bottles, I

got bolder. I swapped my everyday tissues for one of those square, flowered boutique boxes of colored ones. Nothing happened. No reaction.

I took a Limoges candy dish—a wedding present I had packed away years before to keep it out of the way of little hands—from the storage closet and set it on the new dresser, filling it with lipsticks, hairpins, and combs, just as my mother and Sam's had done so many years ago.

It was the afternoon after I had put the lipsticks in the dish that Rebecca finally said something. She came into our room where I was sewing and just looked. Then she said, very softly, "Could I please see your lipsticks?" She who, as recently as the day before yesterday, had been death on lipsticks was suddenly asking, and asking with a near reverence.

It was her reverence, of course, that told me what was happening. "Yes, you may."

She took a tube, opened it, looked at herself in the mirror, and then closed the lipstick, saying as she screwed it back down into its tube, "I guess I'll wait awhile." Then, "I'll just take some lotion instead," but she didn't. She just stood there a minute or two more considering herself in the mirror, and then without saying anything else, she left.

Over the seven years since then, I have added a set of makeup brushes that I have never used because I don't know how, but I bought them because of the richness of the feel of the case they are in and because of the flower cart that is depicted so exquisitely on their top. I also have added one of those elegant sets of Chinese stacking boxes to hold my favorite necklaces. I chose the set not for its usefulness, however, but because its serene designs and brilliant lacquered red make me happy with life and Asian luck.

There are times now—many times, in fact—when I just sit in the sewing chair and rock, looking at the dresser with its icons of perfumes and crèmes, its vessels of pins and baubles, its simple cloth and lacquered reliquary. I rock and look and am always more and more at one with the new life that began with the ordering of the dresser, more grateful for the slipping into things that this altar gave me.

Going forward into what my mother was when I first remember her, and watching her granddaughter work to become us both, I disappear into creams and odors and pins just as, from the beginning of the whole thing, I think I must have known that I would. When by the grace of God the things that became the symbols become things once more, neither they nor we are the same, nor have we changed. It is the use of even the simplest sort of icon to teach us that, I suspect.

AUTUMNAL

EMBER DAYS

Historically the ember days were always observed four times a year. They fell on the Wednesdays, Fridays, and Saturdays immediately after (1) the first Sunday in Lent (spring); (2) the Day of Pentecost (summer); (3) Holy Cross Day (autumn); and (4) December 13 (winter). Over the decades of this century, however, Ember Days—probably, I always thought, because of the autumnalness of their name—have been most actively observed in the fall of the year. As a result, most of us, if asked when Ember Days are, will now respond with "in the fall," remembering only after the fact to include the spring observance and almost never remembering to mention the summer and winter ones.

As an omission or a diminishment of the liturgical calendar the loss of the Ember Days never really troubled me much until recently because they never really treated of anything that had been privately and emotionally important to me. Simply put, the Days are dedicated to prayers for the clergy—to thanksgiving for them, to petitions for their increase, and to requests for their spiritual sustenance. Since, until recently, I had never had to experience the Christian life without a pastor, I had never had any depth of appreciation or concern. That has all been changed now.

8.

HOW BEAUTIFUL UPON THE MOUNTAINS

WE HAVE A NEW PRIEST IN OUR PARISH...
or if he's not new, he still feels new. He has been
with us for almost a year now, so his recentness is
debatable, I suppose, but our perception of it is certainly incontestable.

Most of us had never been without a pastor before.
Midway of the ten months that we were unpastored,
I took an informal poll after services one Sunday. I
had to know if I were the only one in the place who
found ours to be a distressing situation. I was relieved to discover I was not alone—most of us had no
idea of how to run a parish without a priest and
absolutely no prior experience to draw on for help,
especially not in a fairly small and fairly rural parish.

The usual and obvious things happened on sched-
ule, of course. I mean the lights were on, so apparently the junior warden was paying the bills. Bill Bains's
elaborate spice garden and flowering borders continued to thrive in the churchyard. (They are oblivious
to the need for any blessing except the ones that fall
on them constantly from Bill's hands, I suppose.)
There was always at least one service each Sunday, so
either the senior warden or the bishop must not have
forgotten that we existed.

I never did figure out who was doing our burying
and our marrying because, selfishly but fortunately,

neither we nor anyone I knew had occasion for either function. (Country parishes are rather healthy in the long run and not much given to hasty marriages. If my memory serves me correctly, however, the new priest performed three weddings in the first month after his arrival, but that is beside the point.) Baptisms we did on Sundays with the interim preacher of the day serving as officiant. Since baptisms are so poignant in and of themselves, I have always held that who the officiant is matters almost not at all.

But despite all the apparent routine and the surface tranquillity, things began to change for us in those ten months. The size of the congregation dwindled more each Sunday, as did the size of the choir until it got down to a soloist for a Sunday or two toward the end of things. Since no one I know really goes to church to see the preacher, I found this diminution hard to explain. Yet I, too, felt its pull, its call to lie dormant because the parish felt dormant; illogical, but alarming in the power of its lassitude.

Holy days were not kept. For the first time in my adult life, day after day peeled off my kitchen calendar uncelebrated and unmarked save by private prayer at home. Wednesday nights the only church lights were the arc lights in the parking lot. Daily offices went unsaid. Literally we fainted and were scattered abroad as sheep having no shepherd, a piece of Scripture that I never had appreciated until I had to watch it happening around me.

Then he came. How beautiful upon the mountains the feet of them that bring glad tidings—another piece of Scripture that I never had really appreciated until I got to watch it happening around me.

It was gradual, you understand. No major events, no dancing in the parish hall. It was all very quiet and very subtle. The first thing I noticed actually was almost inconsequential. Grown men, all of them perfectly capable of having acted on their own without direction, suddenly decided one Saturday to spend the afternoon trimming the edges of the parking lot and poisoning the grass that over the past few months had broken its way into the asphalt in at least two dozen places. *Interesting*, I thought, *that none of us had seen it all summer or worried about it*.

The next thing I knew there were people I had never seen before coming to Sunday services. Where he found them I may never know. Although I know many of them now, I can't imagine just outright asking someone, "Where were you when he found you?" much as I would like to.

Then the back row and shortly after that the two back rows (we're working on the third one now) began to fill up with babies, or with families with babies. If you sat anywhere in the back third of the nave, you were destined not to hear any single sermon in its entirety. You did gain, however, an overwhelming sense of our future as a body of God's faithful.

The next thing was that the holy days came back, not only the big ones that we were accustomed to having but also the little ones that we weren't, the so-called lesser feasts and fasts. Six weeks into the new cleric, one of my friends in the Altar Guild sighed to me as we were leaving services one evening, "My goodness, he's going to church us to death!" I looked at her, and we both laughed out loud like those who have discovered water in the middle of a drought.

Or maybe I should say food in the middle of a famine. I had truly not realized how derelict we had become about the transient poor and homeless until the parish kitchen began once more to fill up with donations of canned goods. And I had forgotten how much I despised those tacky containers that sit on our supper table and say "Pennies for Hunger" until Rebecca triumphantly set one there about six months ago and said, "See what we've got again!" And it is still fed more by her change and allowance than by anyone else among us, so great is her pleasure in once more having a priest to collect and use it. So the changes have occurred, and we have rejoiced.

I had occasion to drive to the cathedral two weeks ago and was greeted by the bishop as I went in the narthex door. In passing, he asked me how I liked our new rector, and I heard myself responding, "Just great, but it's a little like watching the Roto-Rooter man at work." He looked a bit nonplussed and I certainly felt it, but I knew I had said, albeit unthinkingly, exactly what I meant. Debris and obstacles and inertia just aren't there anymore.

My metaphor came back to me yesterday when I went to morning prayer and saw the hole in the back wall of our parish house. It certainly looked like a Roto-Rooter had hit it. In truth, it turns out that the vestry has approved the funds to expand the parish hall now instead of later; it appears that we have outgrown the present one rather dramatically and way ahead of their previous projections.

Yes, Lord, I thought to myself, *we do indeed have a new priest at our house.* And this Ember Day it won't be hard at all for me to pray for more of the same. How beautiful upon everything everywhere are the feet of them that bring good tidings; that publish peace; that say unto Zion, Thy God reigneth! Especially of Roto-Rooter men.

SEPTEMBER 29

ST. MICHAEL AND ALL ANGELS *

ALWAYS REFERRED TO AT OUR HOUSE BY ITS shortened name of Michaelmas, this is still my favorite holy day even in my adulthood.

There is something glorious about the fall in and of itself. It demands almost nothing of us except our applause. Save for putting up the hay and gathering in the last of the vegetables for preserving, the hard chores are done until the first freeze comes. The world is still warm, but it's comfortably so for the first time in months; and the chilly evenings speak only of the exhilaration of winter, not of its risks and dangers. So there is in Michaelmas the kind of natural stimulation of the senses that has always pleased me anyway.

But then suddenly, right in the safety of those warm days, cool nights, and lightened work loads comes the most perplexing and titillating set of questions in orthodox Christianity. What is the nature of the angels? What is their use and place in the scheme of things? What is their relationship to us? What is their ordinary and customary dwelling? Christ

*The Anglican community celebrates the angels, both named and un-named, on one day. Roman and Orthodox Christianity separates these categories into two celebrations.

certainly refers to them again and again as active agents in His world. Christian after earnest Christian within my own acquaintance as well as outside it has certainly tried to deny them any function in his or her world. In fact, the majority of Christendom celebrates only St. Michael on this day; the Anglican church adds "all angels." So what of angels?

Uncomfortable with them and yet convicted of their scriptural basis, most of us approach each Michaelmas hoping more for enlightenment than for anything else, I suspect . . . and reveling in the sweet excitement of knowing we won't receive it, at least not directly, immediately, or tangibly.

9.

OF BULLS AND ANGELS

THE LATE SEPTEMBER SUNSHINE, BENIGN AND dry, glowed quietly over the yard and the meadows beyond as we drove into the drive and parked. Like the children, I was looking forward to this week of interrupted routine, of holiday from all the schedules and chores that I should follow—but don't, whenever escape is possible.

We had just put Sam on the airplane for a week of meetings in Boston. For me that meant supper would be sandwiches, not an entree and vegetables—fifteen minutes not ninety, in other words. Time to read. Tomorrow night, frozen dinners. Monday night? We would see how we all felt by then.

For the two boys it meant a definite laxity about the grass. Wait until Friday to cut it again; it doesn't grow all that fast in September. A certain casualness about the hens' nests; they can run a week without new pine needles. A tendency to let the last of the okra get too large to be worth picking, the peppers too red, the eggplants too wormy. A lot of fishing down at the pond, however. Now there was the crop that needed to be garnered while there was still time!

For Rebecca, the youngest at age nine, the prospect was less heady. She alone faced the next six days with hesitation. Our chores and routines were not

yet her burdens; rather they were the definitions of
her days. Daddy's big hands and hearty hugs, like his
long talks with her while they planted and pruned
and harvested, were the mirrors in which she saw
herself as engaging, accomplished, precious beyond
all other things in life. And I, remembering from
past experience, knew that after the sandwiches had
been eaten and the book enjoyed for an hour or two,
those intimate hours of the night would come, and I,
too, would be as morose as she and for much the
same reasons.

So we parked the car, and ideal day or not, we
went into the house. I to wash up the breakfast mess
we had left to get to the airport on time, the boys to
fall dead in sleeping bags in front of the Saturday
morning TV. Only Rebecca veered off to the field.
Like Electra mourning, I thought to myself as I
watched her through the kitchen window. She
wandered aimlessly along the fence line, crawled
through finally, and started toward the pond. I finished the dishes and was thinking sinfully of skipping
the laundry in favor of a manuscript I was working
on, when I saw Rebecca come back over the hillock
from the pond. "Something's wrong with Saint's calf,"
she said as she came in the back door. "It's just
standing at the pond bawling."

"Oh, I wouldn't worry about it," I answered. "She's
just looking for her mama to feed her."

"I don't think so," she said, with the kind of calm
that I have long since learned to believe instantly
when it occurs in children. I looked at her and then
looked out toward the pasture. As I watched, I saw
cow after cow move laboriously over the crest of the
hillock and come to stand at the fence, looking

toward the house. That also is a gesture that years of living with them has made me respect in animals. There was something wrong, or they would not have come for us.

I called for the boys, both of whom protested viciously that this was supposed to be their free Saturday. "Give us a break, Ma" was the chorus, but there was to be no break.

The cows parted as the four of us climbed back through the fence, following the bawling of the calf as it led us toward the pond. Halfway down the sloping pasture stood the calf. Two weeks old and a beauty. Much too old and pretty, I suddenly realized, to look wobbly and weak. Something was wrong. What Rebecca had sensed intuitively I could give adult reason to: that calf had not been fed in at least twelve hours. Beside me I heard fourteen-year-old John mutter, "Oh, boy," and I knew that he had reached the same conclusion.

Behind us the herd had reassembled, waiting for something. The calf began to move, and Rebecca started after her. "Wait!" I grabbed her arm. "Let the calf go." We watched her as she wobbled off toward the east meadow below the barn. Slowly the herd began to break and follow. We did likewise. And there, on the rise just beyond the cow path to the feeding racks, lay Saint on her side; legs stuck stiffly out in front of her; eyes open; flies already eating around her face. As we watched, the calf walked over and tried once more to nurse the stiffened udder. The herd moved off, as if totally disinterested now that we had been led to the spot. *Like gossips, they just love a tragedy!* I thought bitterly to myself as I began to figure dully what all this meant to our intended holiday.

The first necessity obviously was to get some milk into the calf. I sent John back to get some rope, and Sam, Jr., and Rebecca to open up the smallest stall in the barn and get some hay spread out. It had been three or four years since I had tried to manhandle a calf. I had forgotten how hard they can kick and how tough a ride it can be to hold one. This one might be weak and young, but she had no intention of being caught, much less hauled away from her mother. We finally got her down, her legs lashed somewhat inexpertly, and the whole thrashing mass back to the barn. For two hours we struggled, as one always must, with a calf who did not—most definitely did not—like the feel of the rubber nipple or the taste of the milk replacement that we were forcing on her. Finally she ate enough to allow us to go back in for the sandwiches that did not seem nearly so attractive after all.

As lunch ended, John asked the question we had been trying to avoid all morning. What about Saint? Saturday and no one to call for extra help. Leaving her where she was would bring the coyotes and wild dogs up from the Loosahatchie Bottoms and into the pasture. Once there, they would kill the calves as soon as they had finished the carcass. Burying her would be impossible without the backhoe that none of us could operate. I thought of Boston and meetings and wondered how we could have been so foolish as to look forward to this week without structure. Well, obviously we had to move her. I remembered that once Sam had disposed of a yearling by taking the body down to a natural depression at the foot of the

meadow where the close began, setting it in the
little eroded valley just at the edge of the uncleared
bog. We still wouldn't be strong enough to dig
sufficient earth to bury her, but we could at least get
her half-buried and away from the vulnerable younger
cattle, assuming we could contrive a way to move her
there.

Back to the field we went, John driving the pickup
ahead of the rest of us. He negotiated the terracing
and hills with a skill far beyond that of most boys his
age, and I felt not only the swell of pride that comes
to women who have produced good male children,
but also the sense of wonder that recognizes—abruptly
and humbly—that those skills were not self-taught.
They were learned, acquired, taught by the man
who, absent in Boston, was still working the pasture
with us at that very moment. *The eternal line of
maleness, unbroken and unbreakable,* I thought to
myself, as I watched him back the truck up and
begin to maneuver it into alignment, back bumper
even with the outstretched legs of the carcass.

Suddenly over the rise I saw the bull move heavily
and forcefully up the slope and toward the truck.
Long since turned into a useful pet, loved on, stroked,
scratched upon every occasion, the bull was certainly
nothing to be concerned about. John continued to
move the truck as the bull moved deliberately toward
us. A little uneasy somehow, I picked up Rebecca
and told Sam, Jr., to jump into the bed of the truck.
Still the bull came toward us. I called to John to pull
away—"Give him room!" John pulled the truck down
twenty feet or so from the cow, parked it, and
crawled into the truck bed with his brother. I slid
Rebecca back down to the ground beside me. What-

ever this was all about, there was no danger to us if we were still.

Solemnly over the hill came the rest of the herd. I backed off farther, holding Rebecca's hand as we watched. The herd stopped at the top of the ridge, watching the scene below them. The bull approached Saint, running his nose along her now distended underside. He snorted the flies off her head, walked around her full circle once, and then began ritually to mount the carcass. She was too long dead, of course, to admit of penetration and the effort was not that which usually accompanies mating. It was, ultimately, ritualistic.

Farm children learn early the purposes of sex; they also learn early to reverence the emotions of it. All three of ours watched with quietness—not a word said in the whole meadow—while the bull dismounted and stood to one side. As we watched, he raised his head and looked across the fields with a magnificence that becomes a king. Coal black and polished by the fall sun, he uttered a sound I had never before heard from a bull, a kind of call to the herd that was summons, explanation, and completion. Then, as simply as he had begun, he lowered his head and moved on toward the close.

For whatever reason—and I shall never know what it was or what set of peculiar circumstances had contrived to permit it—for whatever reason, we had been witness to something that, I have since learned, few farmers are ever allowed to see. Like Jacob on the fields of Luz, we had watched the customs and conventions of a life as complete as our own; one with which for years we had shared daily space and purpose, but one which we had, until that afternoon,

never seen. Like Jacob, too, we knew we were on
holy ground. We had been in Bethel; we had been
witness to the mysteries of another order. Through
the tears in my eyes, I looked down and saw Rebecca
swipe at hers with her forearm.

The herd slowly came down the rise toward us.
Most of them paused to smell the carcass with their
lowered noses; they all moved toward the bull, still
waiting for them in the shade of the close. Once
there, they followed the way of cows and settled
down to doze in the fading sun as if nothing had
happened. The bull alone stood watching us.

Without asking, John swung back over into the cab
and cranked the motor. Adroitly he put the truck
back into position and lifted out the lengths of rope
he had brought from the barn. Together, with Rebecca
and Sam, Jr., watching, we lashed the stiffened legs
together and then to the hitch on the back of the
truck and began the tedious process of inch by inch
dragging the body down to the edge of the bog. With
nothing said, Sam, Jr., picked up a pole, and the
three of us, once the body was unlashed, rolled the
last of Saint down into the gully below.

Rebecca and I walked back to the house while the
boys finished and parked the truck. Without thinking, I began to chop salad and season a quart of
beans. There would be leftover fried chicken, and I
could throw some biscuits in the oven... *an entree
and vegetables*, I thought to myself. Sam, Jr., came
in and silently picked up the garden basket. I saw
him a few minutes later picking the okra in the
garden. Far to the front I heard John turn over the
motor on the lawn tractor. We would have a trim
yard for Sunday after all. Supper would be ready in a

little while, then baths and to rest. Tomorrow would
be Michaelmas—the Feast of St. Michael and All
Angels—the one day of the year when all Christendom pays at least lip service to invisible realities
and unseen orders. We who had been so subtly in-
structed would likewise be ordered and ready when
the words of the Prayer Book began tomorrow
morning's worship: "O Everlasting God, Who hast
ordained and constituted the ministries of angels and
men in a wonderful order..."

OCTOBER 4

FRANCIS OF ASSISI, FRIAR

STILL NOT ADMITTED TO THE STATUS OF RED-letter "saint" outside the Roman church, St. Francis is, nonetheless and hands down, still the best known and most loved of Christian saints, even among non-Christians.

Born in A.D. 1181 or 1182 to the Bernardine family of Assisi in Italy, John (his baptismal name) early developed such a passion for the troubadour songs and elaborate ways of French culture that he soon came to be known as "Il Francesco," "the little Frenchman," a name that was to stick with him for the rest of Western time.

Though in conversion and rapture the little Frenchman lost his absorption with Gallic luxury, he never lost his sense of wonder in the natural world or his exquisite union with all his Father's creatures and creations. In a rural parish like ours, as in many a city one as well, St. Francis stands in blessing near the narthex door.

And in our parish as in a growing number of parishes across America, on this day the children come, bringing with them their pets, for the services that always conclude with, and are occasioned by, the Blessing of the Animals. Only King David himself ever had as keen an understanding of the interface between Creator and Creator's world . . . unless it is the children whose pets the priest is blessing on this autumn day. Yet it is a union that I can remember feeling and that country living sometimes grants me again on brief occasions.

1 0.

HAYING

W<small>E'RE HAYING THIS WEEKEND. IT IS A TASK</small> that changes almost not at all from one autumn to the next, or from one generation to another. Seven hundred fifty bales that were scattered over the ground on Friday will, by nightfall Sunday, be tightly wedged and stacked into the loft, the empty paddocks, and the side corridors of the barn.

One of the older children, still single but living now in the city, has come home for the weekend to help drive the trucks. A neighbor from around the bend has brought his truck and his son. They will also spend the whole weekend here, working alongside the two hired hands, my husband, and my sons.

The only real difference between our weekend and the haying days of a hundred years ago is that our hay is bought and hauled in rather than grown on the place. Land is too costly now for most of us to be able to use it for growing feed. Frequently the hay is bought from the acreage along the interstates or from the grasslands under antennae and electric lines or from the fallow pastures of absentee landlords. Ours this year is coming from around a radio installation on the edge of the city.

Day labor as always is contracted on the side from among the men who follow the balers in the hope of picking up a day or two of extra work over the weekend. Most of them are men who grew up in the country and came to town to work in jobs at factories or on assembly-lines. They follow the balers as much for the chance to engage in remembered physical tasks and to acquire fresh produce from the farmer's garden as for the extra money they will earn. Sometime this weekend I will manage to get out to the garden and harvest enough bell peppers, hot peppers, eggplant, and okra to satisfy them and their families for the three days' work. It will be the one pleasant task of my weekend, for like my grandmother and my great-grandmothers before me, I will spend the three days—except for the stolen moments in the garden and the few hours of sleep—in the kitchen.

Again this year I will have unremitting company there as well. The ten-year-old is still too young and too petite to go out in the fields while the trucks and the men are moving the bales, so she is confined all weekend to the house and to the parameters of my eyes and ears. Like me, she will grow cross and restless as the hours wear on. Eventually, we both know, there will come the last run late on Sunday afternoon when Daddy will come for her, and she will ride the trucks in for the last load. Later she will sit triumphantly on the hood of the truck while the men force the last few bales into the bloated paddocks. Until that magic hour of privilege comes, she is stuck indoors with me, and she knows it. We both will pay the price of her sense of being excluded.

By ten o'clock on Saturday I am already making the fourth pitcher of iced tea and uncapping the fifth double liter of Coca-Cola. The thermoses have just come in the back door covered, like my son, in straw

and mud and sweat. I clean them again, replenish
the ice, pour the tea and the Coke, send out more
plastic glasses, and retrieve the last load for washing.
He waits laconically by the back door, enjoying his
brief rest and the shade, hoping I won't hurry. By
midafternoon I will be adding four or five quarts of
beer each time the men come back with a new load.
They will eat sporadically during the day, never
stopping for more than a provender carried back and
forth from house to barn as they return with loads.

As they pull out for another trip into the radio
fields, I make more ice, wash the dishes, wedge
laundry—the sweat-soaked and hay-pierced clothes
they have changed from—into the machine, hoping
earnestly that at least one load will get dry before
they will need to change again. Soon I will have to
plan toward the fried chicken and potatoes and pies
that we will eat tonight when my husband, too weary
to lift any more, calls quitting time. At midnight, I
will still be in my kitchen, still be cleaning up, still
be making ice against Sunday's needs.

But Sunday is easier. The men are tired, their pace
has slowed, the loft is full, and the hay has only to be
set in place on the ground-level corridors of the
barn. It is not quite as hot today, and muscles that
were tight and screaming yesterday have loosened to
work a bit more. By midmorning the trucks have
pulled out for the second load of the day, and I have
started the first load of overalls. I slip out to the
garden, leaving Rebecca still asleep. I am alone for
the first time in thirty-six hours.

On this day in 1226, in the time of God's year that
he most loved, the little Frenchman of Assisi finally
slipped over into the reality he had always known

was on the other side of all this. I think of him as I walk toward the garden. The luxury of the silent fields stretches unbroken around me from the orchard to the cemetery beyond the close. Only the grasshoppers and my thoughts are at work in the dry, brown fullness of the fall harvest. I move, bucket in hand, among the red peppers. They stand like Caesar bleeding from his fifty wounds, the long slashes of red dripping into my bucket as my fingers pinch them easily from the stems. The eggplants, pendulous as the flesh of old men, settle softly into my palms as I raise them from the low vines where they hang, globular and purple, under camouflaging leaves. They go gently into the bucket, beautiful and asymmetrical in their absurd heaviness.

The okra I always save until last. Here in the rows of this most sensual of plants, I pass back and forth letting the tiny fur prick my arms and hands until my skin grows red and angry from the constant rub of our contact. The stalks snap and bleed their milk as I gather the thrusting pods and then yank from below the wound the leaf that has borne the pod in its upward thrust. The okra is servile in its need to be hurt, and only in its bleeding will it come to bear again for me. I bruise it with understanding as I move across the rows, harvesting and pulling.

The sun is warm and clear, but already I can feel the weakness of its light, the growing distance between us and it. The tepeed beans are bloomless, barren vines now sending only tendrils out for sustenance and water. Grief-stricken, I feel the need to lie down, to rest briefly in the valley between their rows, to let the tendrils crawl across me until they cover me and we sink together into the dying autumn. Like a mournful child, I need to crunch the dry soil into dust and smear my body until I, too, am earth; until I, too, can end with what I have loved. The attraction to the dust moves in my fingers, and I gather it into my hands, to crumble it across my sandaled feet, to begin my own burial.... the trucks are coming. Lumbering and hot, they cross over the pasture terraces, over the ditching, moving toward the barn. The men are halloing for beer, water, tea. I pick up my buckets and move back toward the kitchen, the dry mud still caught in my shoes and on my feet. Not yet, my Francis, not yet.

ST. LUKE

THERE IS NO WAY FOR ME TO SPEAK OBJECTIVE-
ly of St. Luke or of his celebration. I live with a
physician, have spent almost two-thirds of my life
with him, and plan to spend 100 percent of its
remainder with him. That fact alone means that the
patron saint of healing is going to always be seen by all
of us in this household in terms of medicine's most
immediate and visible practitioner. It means that
inevitably we tend to see St. Luke in terms of those
characteristics of personality and of mental function
that we know from experience draw a person into the
role of physician and that also make him or her able
in it.

Even if all of the above were not part of my
experience, however, I would probably still have
some trouble being casual about St. Luke. Most of us
do. Because he was a physician and because of those
very characteristics and turns of disposition that mark
his profession, he was in many ways the dominant
gospeler. Of the many parables of Our Lord recorded
in the New Testament, seventeen of them are related
to us only by St. Luke. Without his educated and
curious ear, in other words, at least 40 percent of
Our Lord's active teachings would have gone un-
transmitted. Likewise, seven of His miracles are
recorded only by Luke, five of them quite naturally

dealing with healing itself. My three favorite miracles as a child are, in fact, peculiar to St. Luke: the draught of fishes, the crooked woman made straight, and the raising for the widow of Nain of her son.

But it is the recorded parables, and not the miracles, that are the best index to Luke the devout physician, at least as I have come to understand him over the years of living with him. Luke alone tells us the story of the Good Samaritan, and the Prodigal Son comes only from him. His is the story of the lost piece of money and the persistence that led to sweeping the house until it was found. His the story of the judge who feared neither God nor man, but gave in to the pressure of a widow pleading unrelentingly her case before him. Luke tells us the disturbing parable of the dishonest steward or land agent, whom Christ praises for adjusting his bills in order to find a place among the children of evil since they were evil. Of the four gospelers, it would be the physician whose sense of reality would understand the religious import of those two. And likewise his is the story of the fig tree that was damned by its owner if it could not be fertilized into producing within the next spring season. And so it goes with Luke.

Nor can we leave him without recalling what must be five of the most poignant words in the Epistles. Paul, approaching death and under house arrest in Rome, writes for the last time to the young Timothy. In closing the letter of farewell, he adds, "Only Luke is with me." Of course he was; he was a physician.

1 1.

IN SICKNESS AND
IN HEALTH

In THE BEGINNING, HER NAME WAS VELVET. SHE was simply "the sick one" before it was all over.

Yet even in the beginning Velvet did not quite fit her. She was not black, but russet, with a white star on her forehead and a white blaze on her left front leg. And her softness, like that of all calves, was the coarse-textured softness of the well-licked and well-tended, not of the supple and silky. Nonetheless, Velvet it was . . . originally.

She was born on one of those fiercely windy days that mark the deep winter weeks of West Tennessee. The sky never got brighter than twilight that day, and the ice flakes blew, like falling leaves in autumn, off the twigs and limbs of the trees in the close. Dolly was her mother and a good breeder. She had brought herself in early that morning, first to the feed lot and then into the open corridor of the barn itself. There was no trouble in persuading her to move into the hay-strewn stall that Sam had prepared for her, and no protest when John shut the door on her. Before supper time, we had Velvet.

By the spring Velvet was as strong and friendly and fleshed-out as all Dolly's calves had been, just a bit more adventuresome. Occasionally, looking at rambunctious Rebecca, Sam and I would laugh about Velvet and reassure each other that the more offspring one has, the more daring they become; but we never meant for our joke to be taken seriously.

Then came the rains of April. Velvet had trouble bending her personality to her environment. All the places that a calf could cavort in or graze on or even just be curious about were muddy at first, then slippery, then miry. Life in the lower pasture was not good. It certainly was not surefooted. And that was how it happened.

There is, between our pond and the first fields of the untended land behind us, a dam that Sam threw up years ago in order to raise the water level in the pond. The structure, put there through days of excruciating labor with tractor, blade, truck, and sheer determination, always stands at least three feet above water level even in the rainy season, and at least six to seven feet above the fence and empty field below it.

The path across the dam, worn down originally by the children playing on it, fishing from it, and racing across it, is no more than two feet at its widest point. But cows are as gullible and as lazy as any other of God's creatures and so, though not surefooted as a species in the first place, before long they began to follow the children across the dam. Shortly thereafter they apparently came to regard the narrow path as a time-saving bridge that prevented their having to go around the pond to get to the upper meadow and Mary's hill. Since cows seem to have nothing but time, it always amused me to watch them line up single file to begin their trek across the dam, its narrowness clearly causing them concern, but the attraction of its shortcut clearly proving to be irresistible.

It was not, then, that Velvet was where her mother would not have wanted her to be on the day she fell. It was simply that Velvet was crossing in a manner neither her mother nor her other kin would have approved of, had they known. I saw it happen, in fact. I was standing at the kitchen window daydreaming about how lovely it was to be dry instead of out in the drizzle and to be female instead of Sam, who at that moment, propped against the doorjamb, was struggling into his boots so he could go do his evening chores.

The minute Sam finally got into those boots and opened the back door, of course, every cow on the place knew it; and long before I heard him clang the chain on the orchard gate, every one of them already knew he was going to clang it. Slowly, as I watched from my warm, dry kitchen, they started that bovine shuffle with which cows always reassemble themselves. Once again turned into a herd, they moved together toward the barn and food—all except Velvet. She was intensely involved with something at the edge of the pond. Dolly was almost out of her sight when Velvet looked up and saw the departing herd. It was then that she tried the impossible. She tried to gambol across the dam. And she made it about four feet across before her feet went. I saw her legs slide under her, watched her roll onto her flanks, and then chuckled as the whole of her, mud and all, tossed off the far side of the dam.

It was when Velvet did not immediately come back up into view that it even occurred to me that she might be hurt. I waited a few minutes and, when nothing happened, put on my boots. By the time I had got as far as the pasture fence, I could see Velvet climbing back up onto the dam. As I watched, she slowly and much chastised made her way across and up the hill toward the barn. I went back into the house, took off my boots, and finished getting supper on the table, giving no further thought to Velvet.

When Sam came in, he was laughing. "What did that dumb calf do? Fall into the pond?"

"No, but you should have seen what she did do!" And I told him of Velvet's attempt to be a colt instead of a calf.

"Well, she's the muddiest thing I ever saw! I got most of it off, but Dolly and the grass are going to have to do the rest."

"Did it hurt her?"

"No, doesn't look like it. Seems to have hit something... probably one of the fence posts... with her right side, but it just roughed up her hide... didn't even break the skin." And we sat down to eat, having no more concern than a good tale to share with the children as they came to the table.

It was at least a month later—the weather had already grown warmer and Sam and the boys were no longer throwing out extra hay for the animals every night—that Rebecca remarked that Velvet sure did look funny. The only reason I remember it is that Sam went out after supper that night just to check, and said, rather casually to me later, "Becca's right. That calf does look funny... sort of malnourished, in fact. But Dolly's got plenty of milk. We'd better watch her for a day or two."

His day or two was to stretch into five months of watching. At first, Velvet was merely weak. She who had always run and played and nipped now lay most of the day beside her mother. She no longer came to

the fence when Rebecca was in the hammock or to
the gate with the herd when Rebecca was in the
orchard picking faulty apples and pears for them. It
was in those weeks of late June and early July that
she ceased to be Velvet and became the sick one. It
was a removal, a distancing, the children created by
themselves.

In the course of his years as a physician, Sam has
talked, from time to time, of the anguish peculiar to
treating the terminally ill. Not because of their ill-
ness or their coming death or even their often intrac-
table pain, but because of their isolation. Because of
the withdrawal from them of everyone—their families first, then their acquaintances and, near the end,
sometimes even of their medical support teams. Probably no part of medicine has been more in his
conversation than this one thing. His frustration that
it should happen; his anger that time and time again
he should have to watch that withdrawal from someone for whom he cared; his rage that he himself
should still feel so strongly the animal instinct to
withdraw and should, after all these years, still have
to fight against himself in order to stay the course.
Now here we were watching the same thing in our
children. No one had said that the sick one would
die; it was built into the changing of her name. They
had loved on and handled Velvet; they only watched
the sick one.

By July, Sam knew what had happened. "The blow
to her side when she fell off the dam. It must have
caused a stricture."

"She's starving?"

"She's starving... not enough getting through the
narrowing in her gut where she hit it ... certainly not

enough to keep her alive for much longer this way."
And he began to mix various kinds of high protein
formulas and pabulums for her. Most of his efforts
only came back up again, frequently all over him as
well as the calf.

Then the bloating began. In her hunger she continued to eat, and the food, unable to pass out of her
stomach, stayed there. Over the weeks of August and
September, her front grew more and more distended
and her midsection more and more emaciated. Old
Buck Jones, the vet we had used for years, just
simply wouldn't come any more.

"It's no use, Doc. You ain't gonna save this one
regardless of how many times you call me out here"
had been his parting shot the last time he came to
see her in mid-September.

But Sam continued his ministrations, carrying the
nursing bottle to the barn two times a day, sometimes three. Then she rallied. She began to move
around more during the day. I even saw her playing
one afternoon with another calf. The distension went
down a bit, and if her middle did not get fatter, it at
least did not get bonier. The children and I were
encouraged. Only Sam shook his head. "She's just
quit eating all together, is all," he said. "And the
decreased pressure in her belly makes her feel better."

By mid-October, it was obvious that he had been
right. For two days she huddled in the barn, lying all
day on the hay in the stall where she had been born.
Dolly no longer even came around her or showed
any interest at all in her whereabouts, nor did the
children. Finally on Sunday afternoon after lunch,
Sam came back in from seeing about her in the barn.
Saying nothing, he moved around the kitchen pack-

ing his pockets with string and matches and even my
baster. "Will you help me?" he asked as he crossed
behind me and got the big butcher knife out of the
kitchen drawer, adding it to his jacket full of supplies. I nodded yes as I dried my hands on the dish
towel. "Come on when you finish then," and he was
gone out the door.

The children were all doing homework, and I was
certain that I did not want their help, so I said
nothing as I slipped quietly out the back door and
followed him to the barn. By the time I got there he
had already taken one of the wide rolls of black
plastic he uses for tarping and spread it across the
stall floor and over the hay. He was lifting the calf
onto the center of it as I came in. She was totally
toxic by this time and unconscious, a dead weight in
his arms. The exertion of positioning her was already
making trickles of sweat down his neck as I knelt
down to help him cover her with the old blankets he
had brought from the house.

"Not much of an operating room, is it?" He laughed
at me sardonically.

"Not much." Even as I answered him, all the years
we had shared together so long ago when he had
been fresh out of school and in general practice in
the country came running back. It had been primitive then, too, those years before residency and
fellowship and subspecialty, before fancy hospitals
and elaborate drugs and elegant equipment; those
years as doctor in a mill village among the incredibly
poor with only his inventiveness between us and their
deaths. I had helped because I had had to. He had
taught me, often right on the spot, and I had loved

the learning and the being together. Sometimes we had lost, but most of the time we had won.

But this time we were going to lose. I knew enough medicine to know that. Listening to his labored breathing as he adjusted her one last time, I said it. "Why? Why are we doing this now?"

"Last week it would have killed her. There's no way on God's earth to anesthetize her, you know that. This week she's too near gone to even know we're here, much less what we're doing."

"But you can't possibly get a sterile field out here in all this mess!"

"You noticed that, did you." His sarcasm was again more sardonic than biting, his mind too much involved in his own efforts to be concerned with mine. "But I'll tell you one thing. If she makes it till I can get in there and there's any way in the world to reconnect that gut around the stricture, we're sure going to give it the royal try, and the devil can take the hindmost!" Obviously, as in the old days, I had just been given my instructions, or as much of them as there was ever going to be.

He straightened out her legs to expose the injured side. Rising, he went out and came back again with three of his clamp lights. He hung them from the tack racks and ran an extension cord to each. Still not enough light to really see. He left me with the calf again. In the corner beyond her he had already laid out the sutures and clamps and sponges that, in all our years in the country, he has always kept in the shop cabinet against some emergency, some injury to children or neighbor or self.

He came back into the corridor, and I heard him rummaging in the toolchest. Coming into the stall, he handed me his portable spotlight. "You'll have to hold it" was all he said before he dropped to his knees again between the calf's extended legs and began to palpate her abdomen. She didn't even stir as his hands moved back and forth, feeling and defining as they went. Never once did she appear to know that we were there, even when he pressed hard over the upper part of her gut.

"Here it is," he said. "Turn on the light."

And I did as he picked up the knife and opened the skin deftly and swiftly. Then, more slowly and more deliberately, watching her for any sign of stress as he cut, he incised the skin; moved through the muscle and fascia, clamping the bleeders as he went; and laid open her abdominal cavity. There exposed in clear view at last were the stomach and the intestines; and between them, just where the stomach empties into the digestive tract, was the stricture, the six or seven inches of dead intestine. He lifted it up, felt it between his fingers, and shook his head.

"Want to try?" I said.

"Can't. Gut's already gone below it."

Looking beyond his hand, I saw the rest of the intestine purple and engorged beyond the spotlight's peripheral glow.

"Damn it all!" The sweat, even in the cold barn, was running down his neck, and his hair was wet from the exertion of opening her and from, I thought, his own intensity.

I watched him as he settled down on the black plastic. Impervious to the feces and blood around him, he began to clean off her skin. "Go get the gun."

I did not say anything, just turned off the spotlight, hung it on a hook, took one last look at him there in between the calf's legs and covered in her waste, and left. I had not gone as far as the orchard gate when I heard the first blow. I also heard the crack as her skull gave way beneath it. There were two more rapid blows and then silence. Standing there with one hand on the gate and listening to the quiet, I remembered that he had rummaged in his toolbox before we began—and that he had had the hammer as well as the spotlight when he had come back into the stall. He had never intended to make her wait for the gun.

I turned and went back to the barn. In the stall he was covering her with the black tarping. The hammer lay near the door where he had thrown it. He looked up startled, still on his knees and his hands still grasping the corners of the plastic, as I came in "I didn't mean for you to come back so soon . . ." His voice trailed off.

"I'll help you clean up."

"No," he said, still on the floor and still working to secure the corners of the tarp over her. "No. I want the children to do that."

"All three of them?" My heart rose to Rebecca's pain in seeing this scene, in having to carry supplies and help clean tools.

He rolled forward toward the hay rack and pulled himself up by it, slapping his thighs and stomping his feet as he stood up. "We tried. We lost, but we did try. And we will also finish it. Don't you want them to learn that from us?"

I nodded because he was right, not because I had the wisdom it took to agree. He touched my arm lightly, looking hard into my eyes. "This is just another part of what they will need to know," he said.

Then, as abruptly as his words, he was gone to call his children.

ALL SAINTS

IF ANGELS ARE PLEASANT FOR US TO CONSIDER in the warm, ripe days of fall, the dead seem somewhat less affable to most of us, especially in the growing bleakness and cold of early November.

The church has always taught the doctrine of the communion of the saints, the principle that there is an unbroken union of all saints whether in this world or out of it; that that community is inviolate; that it is a communion beyond the reach of mutability. Exactly what is the relationship between the faithful dead and the faithful living has been debated for centuries, but almost no branch of the faith questions the notion that there is a relationship. And almost every branch has been amazingly content to let the believer treat the problem in the way most comfortable to that individual as long as he or she didn't get too outspoken or too definitive in any opinions.

However the individual may wish to deal with the dead and/or the ongoing communion of the saints, the church still holds All Saints as a major feast day and still demands of us as believers some consideration of the question of death itself and of those who have passed into it.

1 2.

THE NECROPOLIS
AT OUR HOUSE

At the foot of the pasture, just where the fence meets the bog, there is a homemade stile fashioned years ago of stones and logs by little Tickles seeking easier access to the village cemetery beyond our property line. Although it is not beautiful, it has, as contrivances go, been remarkably effective, having carried more than its fair share of cousins, playmates, and siblings across the fence from pasture games to graveyard play.

Rebecca, at twelve, goes across rarely now, and the boys not at all. But there was a time when even the older children could recite the names and histories of at least three dozen of its dead, so great was their intimacy with the place.

They played originally, of course, without any reverence and, as very young children, without any acquired regard for spooks and goblins. The cemetery was simply another part of our part of the village where another set of neighbors existed—statically perhaps, but existed.

It used to fascinate me that they always spoke of the buried in the present tense.

"The General's got some kind of awful, red gooey stuff growing up his stone. John tried to scrape it off, but it wouldn't come. What do you reckon it is?"

"Miss Pink's flowers are dead. Do you think she'd like some of our marigolds?"

"Sam was cracking walnuts on Mrs. Todd's foot marker, but I told him to stop. She wouldn't like it a bit if she could see the mess he's made!"

And then, as each started to school and began to realize the broadening social world that makes school tolerable (even enjoyable in village schools) for most of us, I was equally fascinated to watch each of them tie their new friends backward, so to speak, to their dead ones.

"I met a new kid today—name's Jimmy Brandon. His granddaddy's over there under that last oak by the corner of the fence. I asked him, and he said it was his granddaddy."

As they grew older, they played less raucously in the cemetery, as they did everywhere else, of course. Each briefly went through a Halloween phase of wanting earnestly to believe in scary places, and of wanting our cemetery to perform that service for them. But as a thriller, it was a washout. After all their years of playing and daydreaming there, the place was too comfortable, too familiar to make their eyes see what was not there, or their blood race. So now it matters almost not at all to any of them except as a storybook loved in childhood but outgrown in adolescence still matters, still instructs, still is part of what the adult becomes.

When she was home last fall for a visit, Laura went down to see about it. At first I didn't know where she had gone until Becca, who knows everything, said, "She's gone to see the General. I saw her climbing over the stile."

When she got back, I was cooking lunch. "How was he?" I asked as she came in.

She grinned, a little sheepishly maybe, but her eyes twinkled as she answered. "Just fine, I think. At least he didn't complain." And then, in typical Laura-fashion, she added, "And I did remember to ask him."

Despite such occasional visits, so badly built a stile would, no doubt, in the normal course of things, grow grassier and grassier each summer for the next few years. It would, in the normal course of things, sink lower and lower with the rains of each fall over the next few years until it would completely revert to the rubble and lumber from which it came. But there are grandchildren coming along now . . . still too little to haul logs and rocks or even to shift those that have already been hauled. As a first social experience with the dead, however, the old stile has certainly been a comfortable one, and for that reason alone, it probably deserves more loyalty from us than most stiles do. At least that's what Sam, Sr., said the other day when he came back in from restacking it. Actually what he said was "Why knock a good thing when you've got it?" but I think it means the same thing.

EPILOGUE

Unlike those who have preceded us, we can now know with our intellects and prove with our theorems that there is no time; can establish that, at the speed of light, time is not, in other words.

The church knows the same principle by faith, and by their faith our forebears honored it. In effect they gave over half their liturgical observances to honoring it, or to the rifts in time that prove it—to angels and to saints, to prophecy and to mystery, to the dead who are living.

In a way, like the season it treats of, this has been a book about something that isn't so that we may more properly know what is . . . a paradox, in other words, within the skin of whose enigma the I Am waits for us to come home.